Is Your Museum Grant-Ready?

AMERICAN ASSOCIATION FOR STATE AND LOCAL HISTORY BOOK SERIES

SERIES EDITOR
Rebecca K. Shrum, Indiana University–Purdue University Indianapolis

MANAGING EDITOR
Bob Beatty, AASLH

EDITORIAL BOARD
Anne W. Ackerson, Leading by Design
William Bomar, University of Alabama Museums
Jessica Dorman, The Historic New Orleans Collection
W. Eric Emerson, South Carolina Department of Archives and History
Tim Grove, National Air and Space Museum
Laura Koloski, Pew Center for Arts & Heritage
Russell Lewis, Chicago History Museum
Jane Lindsey, Juneau–Douglas City Museum
Ann E. McCleary, University of West Georgia
Laurie Ossman, The Antiquities Coalition
Laura Roberts, Roberts Consulting
Julia Rose, Homewood Museum at Johns Hopkins University
Kimberly Springle, Charles Sumner School Museum and Archives
William S. Walker, Cooperstown Graduate Program, SUNY Oneonta

ABOUT THE SERIES
The American Association for State and Local History Book Series addresses issues critical to the field of state and local history through interpretive, intellectual, scholarly, and educational texts. To submit a proposal or manuscript to the series, please request proposal guidelines from AASLH headquarters: AASLH Editorial Board, 2021 21st Ave. South, Suite 320, Nashville, Tennessee 37212. Telephone: (615) 320-3203. Website: www.aaslh.org.

ABOUT THE ORGANIZATION
The American Association for State and Local History (AASLH) is a national history membership association headquartered in Nashville, Tennessee, that provides leadership and support for its members who preserve and interpret state and local history in order to make the past more meaningful to all people. AASLH members are leaders in preserving, researching, and interpreting traces of the American past to connect the people, thoughts, and events of yesterday with the creative memories and abiding concerns of people, communities, and our nation today. In addition to sponsorship of this book series, AASLH publishes *History News* magazine, a newsletter, technical leaflets and reports, and other materials; confers prizes and awards in recognition of outstanding achievement in the field; supports a broad education program and other activities designed to help members work more effectively; and advocates on behalf of the discipline of history. To join AASLH, go to www.aaslh.org or contact Membership Services, AASLH, 2021 21st Ave. South, Suite 320, Nashville, TN 37212.

Is Your Museum Grant-Ready?

Second Edition

Sarah Sutton

ROWMAN & LITTLEFIELD
Lanham • Boulder • New York • London

Published by Rowman & Littlefield
A wholly owned subsidiary of
The Rowman & Littlefield Publishing Group, Inc.
4501 Forbes Boulevard, Suite 200, Lanham, Maryland 20706
www.rowman.com

Unit A, Whitacre Mews, 26-34 Stannary Street, London SE11 4AB

British Library Cataloguing in Publication Information Available

Library of Congress Cataloging-in-Publication Data

Names: Sutton, Sarah, 1961 August 16– author.
Title: Is your museum grant-ready? / Sarah Sutton.
Description: Second edition. | Lanham, MD : Rowman & Littlefield, [2018] |
    Series: American Association for State and Local History book series |
    Includes bibliographical references and index.
Identifiers: LCCN 2017060639 (print) | LCCN 2018013940 (ebook) | ISBN
    9781442273115 (electronic) | ISBN 9781442273092 (cloth : alk. paper) |
    ISBN 9781442273108 (pbk. : alk. paper)
Subjects: LCSH: Museum finance—United States. | Museums—United
    States—Management. | Endowments—United States.
Classification: LCC AM122 (ebook) | LCC AM122 .B76 2018 (print) | DDC
    069.068/1—dc23
LC record available at https://lccn.loc.gov/2017060639

♾ ™ The paper used in this publication meets the minimum requirements
of American National Standard for Information Sciences—Permanence
of Paper for Printed Library Materials, ANSI/NISO Z39.48-1992.

Printed in the United States of America

Mary Alexander
For thoughtful encouragement, steady promotion,
and all-around class as a friend and peer.

Doc Smith
For making sure I learned to raise money so I could
help more museums do more of the things I love.

WITH THANKS

David Grabitske, previously of the Minnesota Historical Society and now of the El Paso Museum of History, and Jen Ruffner of Maryland Historical Trust, for their perspectives on state grant allocation processes, and the intricacies of both sides of the online funder portal. Their deep and broad experience helped me think more critically about this important and expanding aspect of grant work.

And to the clients whose materials have been included here, and all who have given me an opportunity to be part of their marvelous, marvelous work.

Contents

Introduction

"Hello, this is Sarah," I said, answering the landline phone.

A sad voice came on the line. It was my client. "We just heard from NEH [National Endowment for the Humanities]," he said, maintaining the sad tone.

My heart sank; so did my stomach. That six-figure grant would have moved that small historical society *so* far ahead in professionalism and public engagement. It had been a blockbuster of an opportunity. I slouched in disappointment. "Darn, I was really thinking we had nailed that!"

In a triumphant voice, he shouted into the phone, *"We got the grant!"*

I was so thrilled that I forgot I wanted to kill him.

He and his staff went on to transform a dying place known for its cup plates into an exciting and popular museum with vibrant programs. I've been proud of it ever since.

I am so glad you have picked up this book. Proposal writing and grant funding are so important for our field that I regularly wonder why more people don't pursue it as a career. Short of being the director, what role other than fundraiser gives you permission to get stuck-in to any aspect of your institution's work? Grant writing may be only part of your job, but how many other positions get paid to fund more of what they want to do? Not many.

Still, I *do* know why people don't choose it as a career. I never wanted to be a fundraiser either. I wanted to do "real museum work" instead. And I wanted to be a director. The last thing I wanted to do was ask anyone for money. When I asked Dr. Smith, director of the

Colonial Williamsburg Foundation's History Administration program at the time, what was the one thing I needed to be *sure* I knew how to do when I completed the program, he said, "Raise money." I hope my outward response was more appropriate than the inward one: *nope, pick again, and pick ANYTHING ELSE.* He told me that everyone in the field needed to know how to fundraise.

Sigh.

So, I learned. I spent the next two years interning in the three departments at Williamsburg that dealt with different fundraising work: individual giving and corporate and government funding. I was recruited by the development office at the Valentine Museum before my program was over. "Doc" Smith's advice landed me every permanent position I had before becoming an independent proposal writer, and it has kept me employed and growing professionally ever since. I was never solely a grant writer, but gradually it became an important part of my work as a staff member, and then the majority of my work as an independent professional. "Doc" is still right.

The way I learned may be how you are learning: I interned; I talked with peers about what I was learning and what I wanted to learn; I read books; and I stepped in to write proposals at work while still in the membership office and to volunteer to review applications at a community agency when I had a bit more experience. I practiced as a volunteer proposal writer for my local historical society to win local arts council grants for programs. At the regional museum conferences, I went to the sessions offered by the Institute of Museum Services (before it merged with the library agency to become the Institute of Museums and Library Services, IMLS), NEH, and the members of the development and membership committees. Eventually I became an occasional reviewer for IMLS and NEH. I steadily built my repertoire, as you will.

In the museum field, graduate school training has not always offered fundraising training. Even today a program may not require any classes in this critical area. Whether you attend a formal program or create your own learning approach, it is still an indispensable skill. Internships in membership, donor research and management, proposal writing, and special events are great mileage. You may choose to find a writing coach, attend professional programs in person or online, or volunteer on peer review panels. All of them build your knowledge of philanthropy, your understanding of what motivates people and how they relate to the institution, and your grasp of the varied mechanics of fundraising in a museum. Since the culture and practice of philanthropy changes continuously, expect to keep up this learning throughout your career. You will have to because philanthropy evolves just as people and businesses do.

Over the past decades there have been some major changes to the profession. In the 1980s corporate funding was still done on a who-you-know basis, and a single letter to a corporate community officer could get you the annual $5,000 contribution with no strings attached or questions asked. At that time, the Foundation Center's *Foundation Directory* was a huge, hardbound book that came out each year. Private foundations were active but much less accessible to those without personal connections. Community foundations were just getting started, and there were fewer players among the mega foundations compared to today. And there were no grants.gov or foundation portals for online applications. The copy machine was your partner after hours when you could spread out twenty-one copies of the Institute for Museum Services grant application (twenty for IMS and one for the museum) to make sure you had all the right pieces and in the right order. It was not a better way to do things; it was where philanthropy was at the time. The biggest differences from fifteen years ago, in addition to online applications, are the sheer volume of proposals that a funder receives, the extent and professionalism of accountability requirements in return for grants, and the increased importance of a compelling narrative in the proposal.

There are more than 1.41 million charitable organizations in the United States: that's 1.41 million others who could be asking for the same money you are.[1] There are only about eighty-six thousand foundations in the United States.[2] There is no aggregated data on how many proposals the foundations and other agencies receive and review, and still we can imagine that it is substantive. It's not a question of whether you can compete; you *must* compete if you are to diversify your income, expand or improve programs, or broaden your reach. Even if all you want is to remain good at what you currently do, diversifying income and expanding your connections is an excellent way to strengthen your organization. If you shirk this work, you put your organization at a disadvantage.

The volume of applications combined with easy Internet access for almost all applicants has led to the development of the online application systems we now know. They work well enough. If I were a software author or an app developer, I would target the foundation market to bring the user interface—funder and applicant—on par with consumer-style interfaces. One of the best may be with the federal government. In chapter 8 you will read about the newest incarnation of grants.gov, a workspace-style approach to submitting an application. It offers a simplified approach to viewing the full application and understanding progress through the submittal and approval processes. It is a better, slightly more intuitive system, and the instructions are much more user-friendly than in the past. The private foundation funders tend to use software that is likely excellent for field management from the administrator's point of view, but it is definitely terrible for the narrative writing that is so important to a strong proposal. There is currently no solution on the horizon, so you will find workarounds, also in chapter 8.

The outcome-based expectations associated with funding today started more than twenty-five years ago but were reinforced substantially by Congress in 1993 when it passed the Government Performance and Results Act (GPRA), requiring government agencies to create, achieve, and report on specific objective, quantifiable, and measurable performance goals. For historical organizations and museums, that meant many of our grant sources—NEH, IMLS, the National Endowment for the Arts (NEA), and the National Science Foundation (NSF)—had to begin requiring proof of results from funded projects to comply with the law. The idea spread rapidly and broadly throughout granting bodies, including foundations, and among state and local organizations regardless of their association with the government. You'll find material on performance evaluation in chapters 4 and 5.

With increased competition and a shift from personal connection to predictable impact, the greatest change for applicants is increased emphasis on the value of the program and the quality of the proposal rather than personal contacts. Oh, there will always be personal relationships that lead to invitations for proposals or access to specialized funding programs within a foundation or agency, but the majority of foundation and agency funding does not hinge on whom you know.

Most support is the result of a careful alignment of the funder and the museum audiences, purposes, and approach. The intersections are institutional and programmatic, less intimate.

The rise of the power of the proposal narrative has come about as a response to the overwhelming volume of requests, the scope of need, but particularly to the way so many of us now consume and process information through the media as either vignettes or long-form human and nature stories supported by images and data and fueled by urgency. The story it tells makes the proposal memorable and of greater value to the funder. If all the basics are otherwise covered in the proposal, including how it solves an important problem, pursues a promising approach, or reaches a valued audience effectively, then a strong, important story will win the day.

So, the one thing you must know when you finish this book is that demand for funds far outstrips the money available: only the most reliable, compelling, well-prepared organizations, with a good idea and a real need, win out. *Is Your Museum Grant-Ready?* will help you address all the basics, and then share the story that makes all the difference.

NOTES

1. "The Nonprofit Sector in Brief 2015: Public Charities Giving and Volunteering," Urban Institute, accessed August 25, 2017, https://www.urban.org/sites/default/files/publication/72536/2000497-The-Nonprofit-Sector-in-Brief-2015-Public-Charities-Giving-and-Volunteering.pdf.

2. "Key Facts on U.S. Foundations, 2014," Foundation Center, accessed August 25, 2017, http://foundationcenter.org/gainknowledge/research/keyfacts2014/foundation-focus.html.

CHAPTER 1

Understanding the System

Understanding how grant funding works, and how to support that process, makes each of us more valuable to our museums. Whatever your role in grant raising at your institution you must understand and contribute to raising money. Whether you are chief-in-charge (development officer, grants officer, director without development staff) or a helper (the bookkeeper, exhibit installer, program leader, event manager), if you need funds for programs or capital projects, then the best way to support the grants process is to understand it well enough to ask the right questions and provide the right kind of material and assistance.

This chapter starts at the very beginning by explaining what kinds of organizations give away money, and why and how they go about it. It all starts with structure. Since mission and legal structure define funders in the same way they define museums, the first step in finding funding is to learn to choose those that support the mission and structure of both the funder and the museum. Start by locating a copy of your organization's 501(c)(3) letter. This comes from the Internal Revenue Service, and it is proof that the museum, zoo, aquarium, garden, or historic site is a tax-exempt organization. It means that your organization does not pay income taxes or real estate taxes, and the gifts and grants made to it are qualified under the statute as charitable purposes and therefore qualify as nontaxable gifts. Most foundations require this as a sign of eligibility for grants.

If your organization does not yet have an IRS tax-exempt letter and expects to have a budget greater than $5,000, there are two options: (1) apply for a tax exemption, or (2) apply for grants only through pass-through organizations, ones that have their tax-exempt status and agree to accept and manage (financially) a grant on behalf of the institution. This pass-through approach is often an option when your organization is pursuing or about to pursue tax-exempt status but does not yet have it. Some foundations will be willing to accept your proposal under these terms. The local community foundation is the most likely partner to accept a grant on your behalf and to manage it for you. To learn about the requirements for tax-exempt status and how to apply, start by visiting the website https://www.stayexempt.irs.gov. The tutorial is valuable.

TYPES OF FUNDING

Now, before you begin your funding search, let's be sure that you are familiar with the basics of foundation types, giving styles, and kinds of money. Funders will have distinct preferences for, or aversions to, various types of funding: operating, multiyear, capital, and endowment, for example. When you do ask for foundation or government grants, be sure the money you need—operating, endowment, capital or project funds, or program-related investments—is the kind they are willing to give.

Project Grants and Program Funding

Grants for funding projects and programs are by far the most common grants. The terms are nearly interchangeable. Both are for specific time periods for specific activities. A project has a beginning and an end; so does a program. A project proposal may have more specifics, more details, than a program. A project may be conducting the first collections inventory, creating the first digital records, assessing a historic structure, or hiring a development consultant to design your new membership and annual appeal approach. A program is likely to be a series of public events, a new school tour design and pilot, or continuing the afterschool program after school. Projects and programs are the same grant mechanism with slightly different purposes.

They are also likely to be the first grants the organization attracts. This is because they are relatively safe first grants for a funder. They have a clear beginning and an end; the results are simple to measure, and the project or program is likely not too involved, too expensive, or too risky. These grants are like a first date between the museum and the funder: if it goes well, there may be more to follow; if it doesn't, there was no extraordinary commitment made.

Operating Support

The funds to run the organization are operating funds, and grants for this purpose are variously called general operating, core, and unrestricted support. They provide support for the organization's core mission, and they are the most flexible funding available. Having this pool of available funds allows the museum to adapt to changing conditions and pursue inner-directed opportunities on short notice. Every director dreams of these funds; most rarely see them.

One reason for the rarity is increased concerns about accountability. Over the past decade and a half, funders have begun to push for measurable outcomes resulting from grant funding. Rather than open-ended grants for general use, the focus is on project-centered funding. This has severely limited available funds for unrestricted grant support.

There are other reasons, too. In 2003 the National Committee for Responsive Philanthropy (NCRP) convened a meeting of local, regional, and national nonprofits to discuss "the importance of operating support grantmaking." The report of that meeting identified three reasons funders are reluctant to make operating grants. They continue to concern funders: "fear of failure," "infrastructure anxiety," and lack of "exit strategies." Clearly operating support makes funders nervous. If you want to pursue this funding, you'll have to learn to address each of these concerns in your program design.

Fear of failure means not knowing whether the grant makes a measurable difference. Counteract this issue by helping the funder understand exactly what it gets for its operating dollars, and that you will be able to achieve all that you promised. For example, explain that in return for a general operating support grant that funds equal to 250 work hours, the funder will make it possible for the archivist and curator to conduct deeper background research on your five historic structures in preparation for exhibits and celebrations that are part of the organization's two hundredth anniversary campaign. Or another example: in return for a grant for 25 percent of salary and benefits, the educator can complete his annual work plan goals of continued program delivery to forty-five on-site school groups, work with staff and teachers to develop two new learning strands for the Native American history gallery, and refresh the print and online teachers' catalog promoting learning trunk rentals and program sign-ups. Now those seem reasonable and valuable, don't they?

"Infrastructure anxiety" is a fear that the institution is just surviving on grants, that it or its staff members are unreasonably dependent upon the funder, and others, for their jobs and institutional survival. The funder does not want to be somehow responsible for future job loss at the organization and for that individual. You counteract that in the grant application by explaining your plans to fund the work of that position—not the individual—in the future. Perhaps you expect to work with another foundation that is a known donor to such efforts, to create an endowment for the educator's position. Maybe there are two major donors interested in restricted endowment grants that the museum will solicit by the end of the year to support the Educator Fund. If there is no longer-term plan, explain that this grant is important for this work for this year, and that the staff member in that position understands the terms.

The funders may want some awareness that this grant is not a promise of long-term support. They may indicate that demonstrated success is expected for there to be even a possibility of continued funding. Set their minds at ease. Make sure they know what your strategic goals are and how you will meet those goals. Explain what relationships you are cultivating to develop other means of support from foundations or from increased earned revenue. The reality is that museums and other nonprofits will always be looking for charitable contributions to do their work; you can admit that even as the funders hedge their bets. It's understandable on both sides. Good reporting and a good relationship will go a long way toward developing operating support.

Multiyear Grants

Multiyear grants, usually a two- or three-year period, are great security to the lucky museum attracting them, but they are hard to find. After a successful first and second grant from this funder, you can consider making this kind of request *if* the funder guidelines indicate this is possible. Multiyear pledges are most common for capacity-building projects requiring staged development over a few years, or for institutions that have already established their ability to perform on an acceptable, laudable basis. Second- or third-year payments will likely depend upon the achievement of the previous year's performance goals. When applying to a funder for the first time, choose the single-year application. After winning two or three grants and completing them successfully, you can speak with the grants officer about applying for a multiyear grant next time if that is something the funder offers.

Endowment

Endowment grants are as difficult to secure as operating grants because they *create* operating funds. You are asking the donor to give you money that you put away, hopefully safely, so that you can use the interest for general purposes over an unlimited amount of time. This is why these grants are so valuable, but there can be complications. The grant may need to be styled to satisfy donor needs while addressing your institutional needs. Do this carefully. Be sure that if the grant includes naming specifications or restrictions on income use, you consider all the effects of financial and legal implications decades into the future. If interest income is restricted to certain uses, can you reasonably anticipate those uses in perpetuity, or is there a mechanism to compensate for any evolution? For example, though chances are excellent that you will continue to need an educator, in the agreement for an endowed position, be careful to state whom to ask whether you need to redirect funds in the future if the position's purpose or role changes significantly.

Before asking for endowment support, it is critical that the fundraising and finance committees work with the director to establish policies outlining investment guidelines, named gift expectations, and management procedures for restricted funds. If you do not have these systems in place but are eager to begin building an endowment, then consider working with your community foundation to establish systems and manage your endowment. Community foundations, in addition to their grantmaking, often hold endowments for other organizations, providing the same investment management acumen for others' funds as their own. The community foundation will invest and protect the endowment corpus and transfer the earned income to you as agreed. Depending upon the community foundation's policies, it likely will not allow a spend-down of the endowment funds, though some may. If your agreement with the community foundation protects the corpus, this will likely allay funders' concerns about the security of their contribution. To find your community foundation, use the Council on Foundations' website, www.cof.org.

Capital Funds

Capital funds are for defined projects' funding purchases of major pieces of equipment, or for building or renovating a structure. The funds support a physical item that lasts beyond a single program year. The grant, whether or not it is multiyear, will last only for the period of the purchase, not an extended period of use. That finite payment often means that capital funds are easier to attract than endowment or operating funds with more open-ended results. Rarely does a capital gift support an entire project, though.

The scale of capital projects often requires more comprehensive planning to complete them and multiple grants to fund them. Strategy is critical because one major funder may require planning permission, construction specifications, a strong individual-giving base, and a rigorous capital campaign plan to make your application competitive, while another major funder may make gifts based primarily on total impact—numbers served—in the resulting building, and assume you have permissions and plans. Some foundations will want to make the lead gift and name the building; others will want no publicity and prefer to be the gift that completes the campaign. Be sure you understand the donor's interests and requirements and provide detailed building and fundraising plans.

Capital gifts, like endowments, are often naming opportunities. The campaign may convey naming rights of the new auditorium, classroom, or building addition if the gift covers all or nearly all of the capital cost. To protect your organization, take care to set an appropriate price for the naming rights, and plan to cover the cost of maintenance on the capital structure once completed. Since grants do not usually cover those future costs, consider setting a time limit on naming rights to last until the equipment would need to be replaced, or the room or building significantly repaired or remodeled. Then a new donor can name the new equipment or capital project upon making a grant.

Program-Related Investments (PRIs)

Program-related investments are not as common in the arts and culture field as in others. Still, entrepreneurial museums and those that often collaborate with others may find PRIs a potential funding option. These are funder investments, no-cost/low-cost loans that support a project that is likely to generate income either to return to the donor or to reinvest in the next stage of the project. Funders interested in community development, environmental sustainability, technology, and social enterprises will use PRIs to deepen their involvement with an organization and an outcome. The project and time frame will be specific, and the funder may be very involved in (or at least connected to) the process and project. The museum will be responsible for a business plan, and there will likely be a contract. Often the PRI is related to the fundraising process for expanding or constructing a building that will offer increased earned income opportunities for paying back the investment. This is a risky proposition for the museum if the funder expects the money to be returned, because, if the project fails to produce, the recipient owes a debt. However, if the PRI is more of a bridge loan during fundraising, the risk is lower. Usually the funder and applicant have some prior relationship that leads to a PRI.

TYPES OF DONORS

Now that you are familiar with the types of money, let's look at the types of donors. It is important to understand the funder's operating constraints so that you recognize what it can and cannot do for you, and why it follows certain procedures or asks for certain information. Because gifts and grants to charitable organizations are essentially tax, or tax-avoidance, transactions, the organizations that make those gifts and grants are managed closely by the Internal Revenue Service (IRS) and the revenue-related agency at the state level, often the secretary of state. Private foundations, community foundations, and public charities are organized within those guidelines. State and federal agencies are regulated by government guidelines because their funds are collected and distributed through government agency channels.

PRIVATE AND COMMUNITY FOUNDATIONS

What They Are

Private foundations usually have one source of endowment and continuing contributions, such as one family donor or a single bequest. Private foundations must, as of this writing, pay out a minimum of 5 percent of their "investment return" for a "taxable year."[1] The majority of private foundations are independent; the next most common are family foundations. Independent foundations are independent of controlling interests such as families or businesses and function with a broad, community-minded approach. Private foundations, whether independent or family, have a primary source of income from their corpus of funds, carefully managed toward the foundation's goals.

Public charities have multiple sources (hence the "public" in the name), including individuals, governments, other foundations, or fees for the foundation's service. They must also actively seek support from multiple sources to retain public charity status. Public charities publish IRS Form 990s.

Why They Give

Giving through foundations may have a structural basis in tax relief, but that relief is based on expected charity, on giving for the benefit of others. Grants reflect how the donors and funding staff wish to approach philanthropy as a resource for public good. Currently, new levels of available wealth and continuing evolution of public needs create a continually changing philanthropic landscape. To us applicants, the changes are in the new ways funders are involved in project design and implementation and in new funding mechanisms and interests.

Their Process

Because regulations do not govern the internal steps the funder takes to make grants, the foundation makes all decisions about how much to give, to whom, and why. How a foundation distributes its funds is rarely the same from one to another. The funder guidelines explain where it prefers to give money. Because foundations receive *far* more proposals, they must weed out a good portion of the applications they receive. Any application even slightly outside the mission focus will rarely be considered, so take care not to interpret foundation-giving interests broadly, and please resist the temptation to submit an application just in case the funder says "yes." Do not reshape your project to fit the funder's mission or create a project to fit their mission. Your project and institution, and their mission and methods, must genuinely match at every level. As you conduct your research, you must carefully match the funder's giving approach to your institution's approach.

First, make sure the funder wants you to apply. Many of the foundations listed in the directories say "applications not accepted." These funders make gifts to organizations they already know, or to ones that they have preselected for mutually compatible goals, personal knowledge, or a history of support. If you do not have an existing relationship, then you can consider cultivating the funder for a future invitation, but do not attempt to submit an application. Wait until you have a relationship with them and are encouraged to apply, no matter how much you believe you are "right" for them.

Most funders have a website making their giving information easily accessible, but some only publish theirs in their tax returns. That accessibility is a clue to their interest in receiving applications. Generally, if you have to work hard to find the guidelines, then the donor is not receptive to requests. You should pursue the relationship another way so that you can learn about their giving focus and the degree of interest in receiving a proposal from you. The next chapter focuses on making the best funder match based on their giving guidelines, so for now let's focus on *how* the foundation gives away money.

The two main styles are responsive and proactive grantmaking. Responsive grantmaking, sometimes called reactive, is a response to unsolicited requests. The foundation staff and board review proposals as they come in, or after deadlines, and make decisions based on the quality and appropriateness of the applications. The foundation's responsive deadlines allow them to fund institutions within their mission but without highly specific requests for program design or outcome. In proactive grantmaking, the funder takes a more focused approach. There are many tools for distributing money: scholarships and special awards to artists or promising professionals, requests for proposals (RFPs) on specific topics, and program-related investments designed to stimulate capital returns.

In both proactive and reactive grantmaking, foundations can make decisions either as the proposals arrive or in competitive rounds. If the funder has more than one grant category, such as arts and culture, historic preservation, social services, and scientific research, each category may have claim on a percentage of giving for that cycle or that year, or it may claim all the funds for a specific cycle. Sometimes the proportions reflect the applicant pool: if 40 percent of the applications are for preservation, then 40 percent of the available funds may be awarded to that interest area. The staff or the board may also feel free to award more money in one area than planned if a cycle has a large number of particularly competitive initiatives in the same category. The staff or board may or may not compensate for this emphasis with a financial shift in a later round. It is the funder's money and choice; there is no responsibility to announce or explain those choices whenever they are made. Since methods and priorities continually evolve within the organization, the print materials may not share these details. If you cannot find enough information online to be confident, it is appropriate to ask to speak with foundation staff about current interests and how giving decisions are made before you apply. You can neither predict nor control this part of the process, but you can ask questions.

RFPs are a tool for foundations focusing on a particular area of need or interest. The foundation can use an RFP approach either periodically or year-round. Certainly, foundation staff and leaders learn so much over years of proposal reading, site visits, and fieldwork that they develop a sense of what can best be achieved and through which means. By focusing their resources on these efforts, they use their learning to increase the difference they make. The RFPs define a specific need or problem the foundation wishes to address, such as environmental action or community engagement around social issues. The RFP identifies desirable methods and results and solicits proposals from any organizations believing they have the solution. This limits the focus of proposal submissions, which certainly helps foundation staff manage their time but, more important, attracts more competitive proposals.

No matter the foundation format and interests, if you have questions or concerns, and your review of the online presence uncovers a phone number, do call and ask for information and advice. (See the next chapter for a sample phone inquiry.) Asking for advice does not commit you to an application.

Once proposals reach the foundation office, they follow a general path. The staff will confirm the applicant organization's eligibility, then check the proposal for completeness. The staff may read the proposals and prepare summaries and recommendations to share with other staff or with the board. Then the staff will likely meet to discuss the best-qualified proposals as they make the final decision. Some foundations invite volunteer reviewers to participate in the initial review process, collecting the comments and recommendations to share with the staff and board in the next step of review. This may take a month to six months. Whatever the process or time frame, you will not be able to make any changes to your proposal once you submit it. On occasion, you may be contacted for clarifications before the funder makes a decision. These inquiries are neither indicators nor omens, and they may or may not change your funding status; they are evidence that your organization and project are being considered very thoughtfully.

On rare occasions, as you wait for a decision, something important may happen at your organization that influences your proposal. You may get a grant from another funder for the same project and wish to let this foundation know, or you may get an award or new opportunity based on the quality of your work on this and similar projects. When it is really exciting news, you can share this by email with your foundation contact if you believe that it affects the strength or outcomes of the project you have proposed. If it is bad news, you should also let the contact know. Any event or news that affects the success of the project should be shared instantly. The program officer will determine whether to relay this information to decision makers. What is important is that you convey continued responsibility for the project, as appropriate.

Most funders will notify you of final decisions. Those that do not should fall into your last tier of potential targets—they are not as invested in you or in the process as you are, and are not likely to change soon. Those that do contact you, whether they call, email, or send a letter, may not be very forthcoming other than to say there were too many requests for the funding available and that this is not a reflection on the project's value. It is appropriate to reach out to the messenger and ask whether you could have a brief conversation so that you can prepare a more competitive proposal next time. You will find that call script in chapter 2. A "no" is not necessarily a "never," so plan your next application based on what you learn from this encounter. Often the notification includes information on when you are next able to apply. Some organizations ask for a one-year interval between applications; others have no such rule.

GOVERNMENT FUNDING

Governments make grants using taxpayer money to support projects that represent values related to the community. At the local level, funding for museums may include arts and humanities grants, educational program support, special programs to improve energy efficiency or install renewable energy systems, support for Americans with Disabilities Act compliance, and preservation of historic properties or open spaces. This is often reflective of issues at the state and federal levels, with the emphasis changing from one administration to another. At the local level, you will find much of this on your town website and operated out-of-town offices. At the state and federal levels there will be specific branches of the government responsible for the specific grant programs.

Local governments are often a great first place to apply for grants. Just as board members and museum members are your "family" of supporters and the first ones you ask before reaching out to the next ring of individuals, so are your town or county governments your "family" of organizational supporters. That $300 grant for a historical character's participation in your summer sundown gala may seem like a small cash return for the time and effort, but the application process is good practice for proposal writing, and winning that grant notifies your current and future supporters than you have been vetted by your community and found worthy.

Whether the program is local, state, or national, the application process will have clear funding priorities, a formal application process, a deadline, and a group of reviewers to make award decisions. The degree of formality increases as you move from local to national. The important difference between grants from foundations and government agencies is the degree of potential scrutiny. To avoid the appearance of conflicts of interest, favoritism, and poor use of funds, the process is very structured and well described. It limits funder flexibility but maximizes access for all. This means the program officers have an obligation to support applicants as they learn about the grant opportunity, identify a competitive project, and prepare a proposal for submission. That information will be uniform for all who inquire, so, though you should develop a relationship with the program officer, do not expect that relationship to be as personal as those with some of your foundation funders. Still, it is very valuable for creating strong projects and proposals.

Some state and federal agencies have programs, often in partnership with nonprofit groups, where the award is the cost-free or very low-cost services of a consulting museum professional. Sometimes an agency offers free services. For example, the energy office in your state may fund free energy audits and low-cost energy-efficient replacements for lights or appliances. Their recommendations are also your "needs" list for making your case to funders. This is also the case with the Caucus Archival Project Evaluation Services (CAPES) and the Artifact Assessment Program (AAP), both of the New Jersey Historical Trust. The Museum Assessment Program is funded by IMLS but managed through the American Alliance of Museums (AAM). In most instances the application process is not difficult, and the award is not difficult to earn. The bonuses are access to no-cost/low-cost consulting from highly experienced museum professionals and their reports, which will likely give you the needs list you can use to prioritize funding needs and make your case to foundation and government supporters. These nongrant and small-grant approaches are as valid and valuable as cash awards for gaining the resources you need and for developing a track record of support. These programs are an excellent early target for your organization's grant work.

At the state level, you can expect to find in-person and online workshops available for free that explain the program and answer your questions about creating strong projects and proposals. The application process will be an online one, with the opportunity for paper applications only under special circumstances. The agency staff likely cannot help with the submittal software and portal, but they can help you figure out how best to answer the application questions or how to choose supporting documents.

At the federal level, you can expect to find free online workshops—real time and archived—that explain the program and provide information for creating strong projects and proposals. The federal application process will use grants.gov as the online portal, and the program officers can answer questions about narrative content, designing the project, making your case, and selecting supporting documents, but they cannot help with the submittal portal—there is a separate contact number for that.

The Agency Process

Once you submit the application (a process described in chapter 9), there is a set, highly scheduled sequence of vetting, review, and notification. Understanding what is going on can ease your wait over the months of silence. Again, you cannot make changes during this time, and additional information is likely unwelcome. The staff will vet the organization and the project for eligibility, and the application for timeliness and completeness (there is no quarter given here!), and organize the proposals for the peer-review process. If your submission is lacking documents, has documents in the wrong place, or is submitted late, it will be summarily rejected. Otherwise, expect six to nine months of processing time. The proposal is likely sent to peer reviewers—professionals like you who are familiar with the field and focus—for review, comments, and scoring. The strongest proposals often have another level of peer review before the staff collects all the information and makes recommendations to the agency chair. The chair is the final decision maker. If you hear from the agency before decisions are made, it is likely to be a budget question, not a content one. This is positive news, and it may be an indicator of success. Agency staff, given the number and complexity of proposals they receive, do not spend time on budget details unless the proposal has made it through a number of basic hurdles or considerations. When the decisions are finalized, you will be notified of their response. For some agencies, you will hear from a congressperson's office by phone. For other agencies, a program staffer will call with the news. These calls are for "yes," not "no." In both cases, you will get an official notice of the decision in the mail. After the official announcement, you can request review comments and ask to speak to a program officer so that you can understand the decision and make plans for your next application.

For a federal grant, you are most likely to be applying to the Institute of Museum and Library Services (IMLS), the National Endowment for the Humanities (NEH), the National Endowment for the Arts (NEA), and the National Science Foundation (NSF). Sometimes, most probably in partnership with others, you may find yourself applying to the Department of Education (ED), the National Oceanic and Atmospheric Administration (NOAA), or the Environmental Protection Agency (EPA). Otherwise, these federal proposals can be very complex, the projects very sophisticated, the competition very stiff, and the agency processes quite drawn out. They are appropriate once you have a grant track record and multiple years of programmatic experience.

You'll know when you are beginning to be competitive for those grants. You'll have strong project and grant success to refer to, and you will be experienced in working with evaluation professionals for programs and a variety of consultants on projects—all with larger budgets. But let's go back to the beginning and find the right funder for you to start with.

NOTE

1. "7.27.16 Taxes on Foundation Failure to Distribute Income," Internal Revenue Service, accessed October 6, 2017, https://www.irs.gov/irm/part7/irm_07-027-016.

CHAPTER 2

Finding a Funder; Ensuring the Match

It's a Tuesday morning. The director met with the board last night. Fundraising is always a topic, and this time they inquired about expanding institutional support, at least for some projects they would like to initiate. The list of projects is pretty long, and you think the suggested funders are a bit ambitious. Now the project is on your desk with some questions: "What about these funders? Do you have any other ideas? Where do other organizations like us get their funding?"

Versions of this scenario occur monthly across the country after meetings of the board, the executive committee, or the finance committee. These are reasonable questions. Your job is to provide a response that answers their questions and provides the next steps, whether they be institutional preparation, project design, or funder targets and approaches. Let's assume for this chapter that you have been given smart, achievable projects, and that only two big hurdles face you: finding the funder match and making sure your organization is ready to attract grants. We'll talk about readiness in the next chapter. This chapter focuses on where to find funders, and how to know which are the best matches.

FINDING A FUNDER

It's your job (and everyone else's) to look for funders everywhere, all the time. Those skills you and your staff have developed for uncovering and interpreting history will translate beautifully to funder research. You may notice a potential foundation supporter when you read a peer's newsletter, hear a name on the radio in support of a local event, or see a name on the banner at the 5K holiday race. If the name is listed publicly, it is reasonable for you to research the funder and consider whether it is a match for you. When you visit the symphony or zoo, the aquarium or nature center, and other museums, take a photograph of the donor boards to help you remember the names later. Collect these for research, and notice the interesting ways each site uses to honor donors so that you can create a thoughtful, attractive version of your own. For a more strategic funder search, use the resources of your local or regional grantmakers association, and possibly the nationally orientated nonprofit, the Foundation Center.

LOCAL AND REGIONAL GRANTMAKERS ASSOCIATIONS

Begin your intentional search with your regional grantmakers association. There is a useful master list of these groups at https://www.giving forum.org/find-your-regional-association. If your state or region has such a group, it means that the base of funders and applicants is large enough to warrant a clearinghouse of information and professional practice information for funders and applicants. Often the association requires an annual membership to use its resources. In addition to access to a searchable funder database, the association is likely to offer frequent meet-the-funder sessions, training workshops, and networking opportunities that are an important ongoing professional resource. It may provide a monthly newsletter with funder updates and announcements, and it may even allow you to work with the association staff for advice. If you can make only one annual membership investment for fundraising, this is the one.

THE FOUNDATION CENTER

The Foundation Center is a national nonprofit with a focus on collecting and publishing information about funders and philanthropy. The material is primarily national, but in this changing world the international aspects are expanding. The center's training webinars and in-person workshops have up-to-date information and very experienced teachers, and it creates and distributes valuable research reports to keep you current on trends and practices in institutional philanthropy in the United States. If your organization attracts funding from outside the region, and/or partners with organizations outside your region, then sign up for the newsletter and pay attention to the reports and surveys the center shares. You may also want to add a subscription (different from a membership with associated grantmakers groups) to the very thorough and easy-to-use Foundation Directory Online.

The Foundation Directory Online

The Foundation Directory Online (FDO) is a fee-based searchable database. You can buy it for a month or a year. If you have a Foundation Center Funding Information Network (FIN) library nearby, you can visit it and access the database for free. There are 450 of these FIN libraries, foundations, and other nonprofits nationwide that have an agreement with the center to provide access to the FDO and help you find training for your fundraising work. Nearly every U.S. state has one. If you plan to access the FDO through a library or grantmaker group site, or online through a one-month occasional subscription instead of the more expensive full-time desktop access, then you can make the process more efficient by building a physical or electronic file of all the questions, ideas, and search topics that interest you until you have enough to warrant the trip or a subscription for the month. The FDO tutorial provides a time-saving introduction to get the most out of your searches when you are ready.

Sample Search Process Using Foundation Directory Online for a Good Match

When you begin a search in the database, you will likely start searching for grantmakers by area of interest rather than by name. In the Grantmakers section, first complete the Fields of Interest section, matching yours with the options in the field; next select the Geographic Focus, noting that states and countries are options but geographic regions are not; and choose Include Government Grants. There is no longer a search category for Audience on the Grantmaker tab, but there is one on the Grants tab. This may reflect the Foundation Center's understanding of a general shift in top-level giving practice from recipients to causes. Audience match is still very important, but the top-level search starts with program focus and then geographic interests. For both funders *and* applicants, this is mission-based work, so that comes first.

Your search may return a list of funders matching your criteria, but if it returns no matches, try to reword the search in hope of finding suitable options from that query. If you have fifty to hundreds of matches to explore, you should tighten your search parameters to improve accuracy. If you have a few matches, up to thirty, it is worth researching each to confirm or deny matches. In the process, you will begin to understand the language in the database and the differing degrees of matches you will uncover within the search. Eventually you will come to recognize the funders by name, knowing automatically whether they are worth reviewing or ignoring. Please hold your excitement until the vetting process is done; perhaps only a quarter of the list will remain after the full research process. Now that you have some names to research, here is a sample process for selecting worthwhile matches.

In this example, to find a funder serving a historical agency in New Mexico, I searched on *History, New Mexico,* and *Include Government Grants*. It produced four matches. I'll use the funder giving away the largest amount of money as an example. The overview information reveals grants of about $3 million to 140-plus organizations in 170-plus awards. The detail shows that the funder gives significant funds in a year to a large number of recipients, but some get more than one grant in a year. Those are the applicants who have a long history with the donor and may work in multiple areas that interest the donor or may receive operating support grants and project or capital grants as well. You don't have enough information to decide yet, though.

The FDO description of this funder indicates that "history" is among their many areas of program interests, but there are so many areas listed that it is hard to tell what the priorities really are. Clicking on the Grants tab reveals a graph of categories and proportion of grants assigned. History does not appear; it is likely buried within a category, possibly Arts and Culture, which received forty-one grants. A click on that category reveals a list of grants including Historic Preservation, which was a grant to a foundation for a historic hotel. So, this indicates some support for historic preservation, but it is only one grant among so many to other areas. This means there is a match, but not a strong one. Do not pursue a grant for a history project from them. It won't be the same priority for them as for you.

Because a fundraiser is always hopeful, and curious, you are likely to take a moment to corroborate other information about the donor. A click on the Map page shows where grants are made. The FDO geographical focus for the entry showed New Mexico, but the map shows grants to twenty-one other states and the District of Columbia. It turns out that 159 grants are outside the focus area, but 2,822 are within it. Clearly the funder will make some grants outside of the geographic focus, but the distribution suggests that either personal connections between a board member and an applicant or other extenuating circumstances may have led to those awards. The funder will clearly step outside guidelines to make a gift, but this is not something a new applicant should hope for. It may be worth revisiting this funder in a year or so or if you develop new programs or projects that may be more in line with its priorities. So, there's no indication of a strong match, but if this information depicts a generous donor who works in the focus area, it is worth exploring to see whether there are other activities that align with the donor's focus and to simply learn more about the donor for possible future reference.

Farther down the FDO report page is a list of Population Groups, then Support Strategies, and then a section on Application Information. This is where you find out if they support the same audience you do, if they fund endowment or programs or capital projects (or all of the above), and how to apply. The information about applications is the least dependable simply because the funder may choose to change this more frequently than the FDO data is updated, so take care to verify all you've learned through FDO with a visit to the donor website. Database searches are great for locating funders, but the final decision-making information is what you read on the funder's own website (if it has one).

For this funder, a visit to the website provides a much deeper view of the way the organization approaches funding and how its priorities emphasize its purpose. While some websites are simply brochures listing interest areas, deadlines, contact information, and links to an application form or portal, this one provides a strategic plan, a series of priorities, and a description of the research behind their priorities. This indicates how learning and improvement is important to this funder and what work it wishes to support. This eliminates all your speculation for an initial proposal and puts it on your watch list as a potential partner for more complex work someday—work that supports their research interests and takes risks on behalf of the field. For an organization new to fundraising, that future may be far off. In that case, this funder is now a learning resource. By following the newsletter and reading its reports, the funder will provide professional development for free instead of grants.

Depending upon the detail of the website, it may provide as much background material as does the FDO with its links to the IRS Form 990s, and maps and graphs of grants. The maps and graphs are a convenient tool for instantly visualizing a funder's granting interests, but without them, the 990s hold a similar, if less simple, picture. Likely the funder either lists its grants on its website by year or provides links to its 990s. The 990s are public documents, but they are not always made accessible. They reveal institutional balance sheets, and, in varying detail, grants, investments, the board and staff compensation, and contact information. The grants list is usually at or near the very end of the form. Here you can see whether grants to one type of work, such as history or archaeology, for example, are token or substantial. You can identify patterns of giving and indicators of grant size. Here are some examples:

- If most of the grants are in the $10,000 to $50,000 range and the grants to historical organizations are all at $1,000 or $2,500, it follows that an application for a historical project may attract a grant, but likely in the smaller amounts.
- If all the grants are at about $250 and the list is very long, it follows that the foundation is acting as a matching program for many $250 awards made by someone else to those organizations. Without a personal connection, that approach will not work for you. Focus on the next higher level of grant as your indicator.
- If there are many grants and one stands out exponentially at $350,000 when all others are $50,000 and below, it is clear that

one recipient is the priority, and your request should be down below the $50,000 level. (First requests generally are anyway.)

- If there are many gifts of varying sizes and to varying institutions, the funder is making those based on commitments to the applicant's project and request. This is where you follow your instincts. You will want to talk to the funder before applying, but it is up to you to choose the tightest programmatic match and ask for the exact amount of money that supports your work and is still within the range of gifts the funder makes.

What if your search shows no direct alignment but still feels very close? Then proceed with a proposal only after an exploratory call. The section ahead on "Making the Call" will help. You may find that "close" is not nearly as close as you thought, or you may discover a new path you had not expected.

ENSURING A MATCH

There's still more to making a match, though. Funders are people, too—even if they are organizations. When you learn about the foundation's history, mission, who it supports, who is on the board, how it gives its money, and what it likes in return, you are learning about the funder's interests and preferences. The Hierarchy of Funder Needs presents one way to sort through the alignments that may indicate a match. If you start at the bottom and then work your way up, you can determine how strong the match will be.

The first three tiers must match both your focus and that of the funder very closely. Without alignment of these three, you have no grounds for asking for support. So, start by checking to see whether there are close matches between your mission and the funder's. Do not cheat here; make sure the two institutions are closely aligned in their commitments. If they really are, then check to see how the next level, "Location and Audience," aligns. Again, don't cheat; it will cost you too much time to apply based on hope. If you are genuinely not sure about the alignment because you are on the edge of a giving area, or you have an audience alignment but something is a little different in

The Hierarchy of Funder Needs
Courtesy of Sarah W. Sutton and Elizabeth H. Clark

your description of audience, then call and talk to the funder to clarify. That conversation will be a chance to get to know them better, to let them know about you, and to answer any questions you may have about the application.

The third tier from the bottom, "Impact/Effect," focuses on the benefits, not the features, of the work you do. You'll read more about that in chapter 4. The alignment is around the intended results of this work: Do the goals of the funder match the expected results of this project? If your answer is "Yes!" then apply. If your answer is "Yes, sort of," then you need to clarify a few things before you know whether the alignment is strong and if you should commit the time and effort to preparing an application. This is best done by having a conversation with the funder about the intentions of your project and, in the process, identifying where there are shared goals. The shared goals may or may not turn out to align with the project you had in mind at the beginning of the call, but they are the ones you should be asking the funder to support.

The next two tiers are the ones that separate you from all the other applicants. The quality you bring to the project, and the edge you offer the funder over all other applicants, is what gets you the grant award, but *only* if you have satisfied the first three basic funder needs. There's more about "Quality" and "Edge" in chapter 4. Many applicants will satisfy the first three needs, but not all five. The quality of your work, and your professional or innovative edge, is what will win you the grant when there are more applicants than there is money—which is most of the time.

Still, no matter how strong the match, there are all sorts of factors that may not be obvious in the guidelines. For example:

- The original donor's legacy may guide giving, or current research may drive priorities.
- On decision day, the foundation staff's comments may be either absent or powerful.
- The board may dislike named gifts and avoid endowments.
- Each board member may be allowed a discretionary project.
- Recent changes in board makeup may have shifted the giving emphasis.

Then again, it all may come down to familiarity with the project and the people. You don't know unless you know your donor.

You can learn more about the people behind the foundation by searching online at first; then proceed to a call. Check the details on the foundation's original donors. Are they still alive? Are they involved in decision making? Are there others on the board of directors—related or not—who might have decision-making roles? Confirm whether the foundation contact person or staff or board member is the same Mehitable Johnson as on your membership list. Check the foundation's 990 to see whether the contact's address matches your member's. You can use LinkedIn to learn more about staff and board interests and backgrounds and to see whether you have peers or connections in common. If this funder seems like a close match, share the board members' and staff names with your board to see whether there are any existing relationships you can use to learn more about the nuances of the organization and the likelihood of matching interests.

Call to Be Sure

If you are interested in proceeding with a proposal, call before you write, if at all possible. Take your cue to call or not to call from the foundation's official information. The website may provide a contact name and number, or it may discourage any preapplication contact. Any donor information that comes from the variety of second-party print and electronic publications may be out of date, or, worse, gathered without the donor's input. You could be applying for the right program with the wrong audience, or the right project and the wrong amount of money. A discussion with the staff will help you craft a more responsive and complete proposal and improve your chances of success.

When you have identified a likely funder match, use the phone call to confirm the institutional match and identify as many details as possible about the programmatic match. That refinement process strengthens both your proposal and your relationship with the funder. Foundation officers and government program directors are in the business of finding good ways to share their wealth. They want the best matches possible. Your intelligent, efficient presentation is an excellent introduction for your organization. Even if this project doesn't work out, you may collect excellent clues for your next approach.

Representatives of the Community Foundation of Abilene, the Summerlee Foundation, King Foundation, and Tocker Foundation, all in Texas, echoed each other during a panel presentation at an American Association for State and Local History (AASLH) annual conference.[1] "[T]he application should not be our first contact," said Laura L. Duty of King Foundation. Instead, you should "call two to four weeks before the deadline to set up a call to discuss the process." She explained that for an online submittal through a portal, the funder can read the time stamps for all your work on the proposal, understanding instantly if this has been a thoughtful application process or a last-minute submittal. Katie Alford of the Community Foundation of Abilene surprised a few in the audience by explaining, "We can tell if you haven't done your homework."

Your professionalism will be appreciated and will help you when you call and apply. After making sure the funder accepts proposals, has similar programmatic interests, and makes grants in amounts appropriate for your project, prepare for the inquiry call. Start by practicing your elevator-ride speech. This is your thirty-second sales pitch. Develop and practice it before making the call—write it out in case your courage fails you or your mind goes blank. Tell whomever answers, "I'm Sarah Sutton. I am the director at the Haleiwa Historical Society. I've read your guidelines and Form 990 and visited your website. I believe our project matches your interests, but I would like to be sure before I submit a full proposal. May I speak with you about the project and our approach to be sure it is a strong fit?"

Now the listener knows that you have done your homework and will likely let you past the front line. When you reach the program officer, or if the listener is the program officer, explain, "(I'm Sarah Sutton from the Haleiwa Historical Society.) We are considering applying for support of a community restoration project for our historic graveyard. I would appreciate your feedback on this before we submit a full proposal. We work with professional stone conservators to train high school students, adult volunteers, and the town's department of public works in identifying, assessing, and caring for nineteenth-century burial markers dating from the time of the missionaries. Most of the stones have suffered from weather and vandalism, and lie broken or partially buried. The project will take five months and include volunteer training and professionally guided conservation work. We will record and restore eighty-one stones, provide volunteers and town staff with training for ongoing maintenance, cultivate adult supporters of historic preservation, and encourage students to appreciate and protect this site. The project costs $35,000. We would like to ask your foundation to consider $17,500 in support of this project."

With these descriptions of the who, what, when, where, how, and why, it's the program officer's turn to ask specific questions, and then to recommend an application (or not) and what next steps to take. Be ready to answer questions such as:

- Which of your staff would be involved? How about volunteers?
- What are the goals and the outcomes?
- Can you replicate it?
- Would it be better done with a partner?
- Has anyone else done this? (Why or why not?)
- Why are you the best to do this?

- If it involves construction, do you know all the permits needed, start and end dates, estimated amounts, any contingency fund, and will you have to borrow?
- Who else are you asking to fund this?

You may not have all these answers, but it's important to explore them before the call so that you are ready. The more you can answer, the better. For those you cannot answer, the response should be "I don't know—yet."

It's okay to ask your contact how competitive the project might be. He or she will explain that every pool is different but that generally this type of project scores well (or does not). Since the funder has no time to waste reading ill-fitting proposals, you will get a fair answer. If the answer is "You are certainly welcome to apply, but . . . ," then don't apply. If he or she encourages you to apply, confirm any deadline dates and the proper contact information. Remember to say "thank you" before ending the call, and to follow through on whatever promises you made or comments or suggestions they made. In particular, should you decide to submit a proposal, take care to comply with any recommendations made during the call. The program officers on the panel mentioned above expressed astonishment at applicants who would call and speak to foundation staff before applying, then apply for different categories than recommended, different project formats, and even much larger amounts of money than the program officer recommended during a phone call. When a funder shares with you time and expertise, the best way to thank them is with a strong, well-matched proposal for a project that makes an important difference.

NOTE

1. Katie Alford, Community Foundation of Abilene; Darryl Tocker, Tocker Foundation; Laura L. Duty, King Foundation; and Gary Smith, Summerlee Foundation, "Thinking Like a Donor: Down-to-Earth Advice from Foundations on Seeking Funds" (panel presentation, "I AM History" American Association for State and Local History Annual Conference, Austin, Texas, September 7, 2017).

CHAPTER 3

Grants and Institutional Strategy

THE ROLE OF GRANTS IN YOUR INSTITUTION

Let's be clear: Grants cannot, and should not, be expected to supply a significant amount of your museum's annual income. There isn't enough money, and a diversified income approach is far better for institutional sustainability.

Looking at charitable contributions for all U.S. nonprofits in 2015, Independent Sector reports that 71 percent came from individuals, 16 percent from foundations, 5 percent from corporations, and 9 percent from bequests. That year all the giving (individual and organizational, but not governmental) to museums and other cultural organizations was only 5 percent of overall U.S. philanthropy. That is *not* an anomaly, and it *is* an increase. In 2013, nonprofits received 72 percent of their income from fees for services paid by either individuals or government agencies. Only 13 percent of their income was from individuals, foundations, and corporations; 8 percent came from government grants.[1] Those very small numbers should help temper your ambitious fundraising goals.

Grants are a very small portion of income; yet they can make the difference between go and no-go for a project. To maximize that impact, you must be clear about how grant funding fits into your institutional operations.

GRANTS POLICIES AND PROCEDURES

First let's consider the internal capacity needed to manage grants well; then we'll move on to choosing which grants to pursue. Internal capacity doesn't start with finding someone to write the proposal; it starts with creating the policies and procedures to manage grant funds and projects, then moves on to understanding budget ramifications.

Let's start with procedures.

You likely have management policies for your collections, finances, staff, and more. The same rigor should be applied to managing your grants and other fundraising. The grant management or institutional donor policies should cover:

- who from the organization must approve all proposal targets, projects, and amounts before submittal. This is the chief staff officer unless you are all volunteer, in which case it is the head of the board.
- any donors or donor types the museum expressly wishes not to solicit for funding.
  - if you are part of a larger organization, the two entities may divvy up funder targets.
  - if your organization has a specific focus or social responsibility profile, you may choose not to accept money from sources that derive their income from practices and industries of which your organization disapproves.
- the critical importance of using grant funds only within the time frame and for the reasons for which they are awarded.
- that no individual related to the museum should benefit from the grant award outside of normal duties for the museum, such as contract or salaried work aligning with institution mission and as disclosed in the proposal.

The procedures should cover:

- how to record the grant application and response processes. There are many formal database programs available, but most organizations start with a spreadsheet for a record of:
  - proposal submittal and due dates
  - project focus and request amount
  - funder's response date and amount
  - follow-up to a grant announcement (who prepares and sends which kind of thank-you message regardless of whether you win an award)

- ◦ grant report dates if awarded funds
- ◦ when the next proposal can be submitted
- the relationship between a named funder and the organization for promotional purposes based on the award amount. Using a formal acknowledgment process is important for confirming any limits on:
  - ◦ donor's use of the recipient's name, and the recipient's use of the donor's name, in appropriate publication formats (promotional materials directly related to the project, general newsletter and website updates, and identification of named gifts). This prevents the need to continuously promote a donor after the project is completed, and protects the recipient from having to post a corporate donor's logo too frequently or prominently.
  - ◦ length of a gift life such as naming rights. These should not outlast the durability of the named item, whether it's a gallery, garden, or an entire building.
  - ◦ conveying basics such as contact information and the correct spelling for acknowledging a gift. This ensures agreement on proper use and presentation of names, titles, and trademarks and prevents unauthorized use. Some donors wish to be anonymous—and don't forget it!

This simple documentation supports management consistency while providing a guide to incoming staff or volunteers participating in grant work. It is also valuable for educating your governing board. Trustees or board members may be new to fundraising or new to the grants process, and they must understand their role in it. They should be responsible for helping to identify potential supporters; support the cultivation process by participating in site visits or funder office interviews; use their connections to further relationships by preparing introductions; write thank-you notes and updates; and exercise patience during the proposal writing and waiting process.

Understandably, they'll focus on the measurable: proposals submitted, grants won, and total income. That perspective limits their engagement to observing numbers rather than building funder relationships and paving the way for proposal success. So, in addition to sharing quarterly fundraising reports (see chapter 9), tell a fundraising story each time. Explain the history of this particular funding relationship, whether it's long or short, and include the cultivation process, previous and planned application attempts, and any other interactions the donor and institution have shared. By keeping the board updated on the universe of engagement work that goes into earning grant money, you'll be educating them, demonstrating how you need their participation, engaging them as allies, and creating a more productive grants program for your museum.

BUDGETING AND PLANNING WITH GRANTS

Now that you have articulated the policy issues, it's time to decide how to incorporate grants in your budget, and how to set goals. Goal setting for a grant program is very different from budgeting for grants as part of your operations. Since budgeting is more concrete, let's begin there.

Budgeting for Grants

You have a choice to make:

- Option A: Build a budget with specific grant amounts and sources identified along with a commitment not to spend money on those projects until you actually have the grant award.
- Option B: Build a budget with amounts allocated to generalized grant income, and a fluid income allocation that moves money out of one category and into another when a grant can be applied to a certain category.

Museums and historical organizations with grant proposal experience can choose Option B, to budget a general amount for grant income during a year based on reasonable expectations of applications and awards. For those new to the grant process, it is more appropriate to start with Option A, where you delay the outgo to *after* the income arrives.

Are you going to do the project or run the program *only* if you get enough grant support? Then leave it out of the institutional budget, and add it to the operational schedule only when you receive funding. This not only protects your budget but also conforms to the funder's expectations that grant money covers only work completed during the grant period. Internally you can use a budget footnote or a supplementary statement attached to the budget for any projects to be carried out only with specific outside funds. When the grant comes in, the project budget can then be incorporated with the institutional budget. This is Option A.

Are you going to do the project even if you *do not* get the grant? Then include the project cost in the operating budget along with the source of funds to use if there is no grant. If you receive grant funds for it, then at the time of the award you can displace the operational funds already earmarked for this work to other activities without grant funding. Include a note and/or list of the projects and the dollar costs with the budget and plan. If you don't get the grant but went ahead anyway, as the year progresses you'll have to modify your budget based on a continued search for funds for other projects. This is Option B.[2]

For those who like to see both options very clearly, two budget columns may be helpful: one with budgeted items (activities to complete no matter what), and a second with grant-funded projects or project expansions.

Most institutions make the decision on a case-by-case basis, but some do have a blanket policy of only moving ahead once a project is fully funded. It's the director's decision. The choice for an A or B approach that is often the most challenging is when you are considering a staff position where the salary is funded partially through grants. A strategic funding plan sequenced to fully fund the position will improve your chances of receiving grant awards. Still, you have a choice. You may choose to hire someone for the year even if you aren't sure enough grants will come in to fund the position, and then adjust as the year goes on (Option B), or you could treat the employment as a project and contract for the position based on a grant award to fund that project and position. You'd begin the contract only after the award is committed (Option A). This is not an ideal way to support a professional or to complete important work, but very often it is the only way to do so during the early stages of a project or an institution's history. When you are two or three years into your grant experience and grants budgeting, then you can prepare a multiyear budget alongside the long-range plan with more confidence, but it will always be a balancing act, no matter how experienced you are.

Creating Grant Plans

You can smooth out the grant flow somewhat through strategically planning your application sequences among funders and mapping out support for projects as the progress and activities mature. Visible sequencing is important for growing from small grants to larger, more complex ones and for growing from small projects to larger, more complex ones. By planning and sequencing projects and applications, you will be building capacity and credibility.

Tiered Funder Lists

Creating the application sequence requires both an understanding of the potential universe of grants to be awarded and the likelihood of receiving those awards. Begin by identifying your potential pool of foundation funders; then rank them by their degree of alignment with your current mission, audience, and programmatic approach. Those funders that have given to similar organizations for similar projects are your priority list. Within that list, the funders with which you have an existing connection go into Tier I: check their deadlines immediately and schedule those preapplication calls and then submittals. Notice when those grant awards would be made, and map them out according to your program schedule and your institutional budget for this year and next year. Notice where an award would affect your budget and planning. Make a note of it and add the deadline to the grants calendar.

Tier II is that same group *without* existing connections. Check their deadlines immediately *and* put them on your cultivation list. See whether the regional grantmakers association will be hosting a meet-the-donor session including these funders. Check the funder website for any webinars, presentations, or open houses you might attend to learn more about the funder and make a connection. Now you'll have to decide to wait, or not, until you meet the funder to apply. If you believe one of your programs or projects is a strong match, it's reasonable to apply after attempting to speak with a program officer to be sure your application is appropriate. If the funder does not encourage this, just skip the call and prepare a proposal *if* you think it is a strong match. Within this tier as well, schedule likely submittal and award dates so that you can strategize where an award would affect your budget. Since you believe your chances of winning grants in Tier I are better than in Tier II, if you have limited time for completing the grant-writing process, focus on Tier I and manage Tier II as you are able.

Within Tiers I and II you will create sequences of grants. One funder may be a perfect match and a Tier I funder, but the timing might not be right for you to finish designing the program until after the deadline. That may mean you cannot apply until nine months from now, with an award coming a year from now. You'll put that grant in the application sequence to follow the Tier I proposals you *can* submit right now for the program. If the first proposals are funded and you have enough for the project, you will begin right away without applying to the funder with the later deadline. If you don't receive any funds from the first proposals, then by the deadline nine months from now you can apply to the next funder. Often there are two, three, or four deadlines in a year, so another *will* come along. Remember, the deadline isn't the reason for the proposal.

Tiers III and IV are for the lists of "maybe" and "someday." The "maybe" list is for the organizations that you feel should be funding you but you don't yet have the right project, and/or you know they only fund organizations known to them so you have some cultivation to do, and/or you hope they will fund you someday. For example, a local company foundation makes gifts to many of your peer organizations, but the focus is special events. You don't yet do special events because of the manpower and space needed. You know that if the right opportunity arose, though, that funder would be likely to support a new venue and program in the community event scene. Keep that funder on the list so that you don't forget when you *are* ready. Another example is the funder whose name keeps coming up as a potential donor but you don't see tight mission alignment. Its awards to school-age learners seem only to go to charter schools and established private educational programs in afterschool hours. You don't see any indication that it would support a historical society doing this work. Keep it on the list for when you partner with the type of organization it funds or you develop a relationship with the staff and are invited to apply on your own.

The "someday" group in Tier IV is for funders for which you currently lack the right credibility or project to attract a grant. This might be the Kresge Foundation in Detroit, where you know that until you develop those two partnerships with the youth conservation corps and the preservation trades school, for example, you cannot effectively "embed arts and culture in larger community revitalization initiatives" or "engage in cross-disciplinary, cross-sector activities" in the ways that would make you competitive. Not only will you be unsuccessful and your efforts unwisely spent, but applying to a foundation before you're really ready reveals your inexperience, and that impression may make it harder to win funding when you are actually ready. Keep the Kresge Foundation and ones like it in Tier IV until your programs are ready. Then move them to Tier I, in the appropriate time sequence.

Include aspirational funders on the Tier IV list. Is there a major community foundation in your region that funds excellent work and is the seal of approval for effective nonprofits? Then monitor its grantmaking and grant focus, and work toward a three-to-five-year goal of being the quality organization with vital programs that it will choose to fund. What you learn by following their work will likely be very valuable in addition to the funds you may attract someday.

Setting Grants Goals

Once you have a tiered list of potential targets and their time frames, you can set goals for grant receipts during the year. The goals can be number of applications, awards, or money received. No, not every application will win funding, and not every award will be at the amount you asked for. So you will set targets, allow leeway, and monitor the results at least quarterly.

Ideally these goals would be set with strategic plans in mind, but often an institution starts with the next year's annual plan to create a budget with grants. In later years, you can align grants with the strategic plan as you build experience and a funders list.

If you're measuring the grant program's success by money received, then, for operating soundness, it's prudent to identify likely grants totaling more than what's in the budget. You can put all those applications in your grants schedule, but not all the potential funding in your operating budget. There is too much of the funding process that you cannot control for you to be 100 percent confident of a "yes" each time.

Similarly, when you create a project budget with grant income in it, such as the budget you share with funders, enter a grant income amount at about half of what you expect to ask for in total from grantors. In both cases you give yourself leeway to absorb the "no's."

If you're measuring the grant program's success by the number of applications and the income return to determine whether it is worth continuing your grants program or whether you are on the right track, then consider using leading indicators rather than lagging ones to help you manage proactively. If you only measure lagging indicators—results at the end of the fundraising effort—then you will only know *what* happened, not *how* it happened. If you measure leading indicators—the activities that lead up to the goal results you're chasing—you will be able to see what connections there are between efforts made and results, not just the results. The idea is that if you monitor indicators early on, you are more likely to create steady progress, to understand which efforts have the best results, and to learn from the nuances of the grant process to improve your grants program. These numbers are qualitative *and* quantitative. Here are some examples of the efforts, or the leading indicators, you can use:

- Quality and quantity of research records for the number of foundation database searches and individual funder research.
- Kind of cultivation work completed, such as participation in meet-the-donor sessions and donor presentations, number of donors participating in your events, and the number and kinds of contact with the funders that did not involve specific requests or plans for requests.
- Number of funders contacted before an application is submitted related to the request.

You will notice that the number of applications is not included here. It's a lagging indicator and a useless one at that. The shotgun approach of applying to multiple funders in hopes of some lucky hits will give you big proposal numbers (quantitative) but few strong matches (qualitative). A more effective approach is to monitor and measure the careful work you do to identify and connect to funders in the lead-up to proposals.

The lagging indicators are the responses:

- "no" with no personalization
- "no" with personalization and, possibly, encouragement
- "yes" with partial funding
- "yes" with full funding
- total grants submitted and resulting income

As your grant-raising program evolves, your goals will change, and your interpretation of the indicators will change as well. At first, higher submittal numbers will feel good, but the likelihood of negative responses and low-income numbers will be frustrating. You might, instead, set a more conservative goal of a handful of proposals and a 50 percent success rate so that you can practice your skills, learn from the process, and create some income plus credibility. Then you can expand the number of applications while raising the goal for the number of "yes" responses. Review your performance compared to goals each time a proposal is awarded or turned down, quarterly at a minimum. You can adjust to reflect changes in opportunities and priorities, staffing, and the general funding environment. For example:

- If a funder bumped your proposal to the next cycle because it was running out of money for this fiscal year, then you should review your budgets and schedules to see whether you must compensate now or wait to see.
- If all of the applications to support the new first-person interpretive programs for the summer were fully funded, then are you going to ask the funder that sent the latest check to fund additions to the program, or will you return the money? (I recommend the former.)
- If all the funding for that summer program was completed before you approached the last funder, then review whether you should delay the application to this funder until next year for the following summer's program, find a new project to apply for, or submit the proposal for the same program but enlarge the budget and increase the program goals for the proposal.

The process of balancing the grant line in the budget with the available funder targets and the priority projects is a constant set of adjustments. There is science and art to it; give it a chance to develop, and give yourself a chance to learn how it works for your organization.

ALIGNING PROPOSALS WITH STRATEGIES

Your planning strategies and sequences should reflect the maturity of the project, the maturity of the institution, or a sequence of needs and goals as set out through assessment or strategic plans.

Projects

Earlier in the chapter we reviewed tiers of funders and sequencing of applications based on funder/project/institution alignments and then scheduled according to next-up deadlines. There are also sequences of projects or programs (from simple or new to mature or sophisticated), and tiers of funders over the years of a project's life. Plan your grant strategy to support the development of these programs as part of the museum's strategic work. Table 3.1 provides an example of how a timeline of planning and implementation might look for your organization conducting a major project. This format is transferable to the application narrative that describes the history of the project.

Table 3.1.   Five-Year Plan for Implementing a Major Project

Activity	Year 1	Year 2	Year 3	Year 4	Year 5
Master plan review					
Community conversations for master plan, then exhibits					
Exhibits design and prototyping					
Program development and research/collections preparation					
Campaign					
Exhibits construction					
Opening and programming					

Tiers

Now let's start with tiers for projects. The goal is to align the scope and scale with the appropriate funder. The audience, the degree of impact and reach, and the level of the messaging must also all align between the project and funder. As you continue to research potential foundation supporters, you will learn to natually align them with matching projects, but you may have to remind board members and colleagues of the importance of tiers of funders and that sometimes you must save a funder for the future. Tier I is likely to include the projects that are simple, safe, and local, and the funders who value those characteristics. Tier II may include the more complex projects, funders interested in more responsive and perhaps risky programming, and projects that have an audience beyond the local and a deep-dive into a topic or activity. Tier III may be your most sophisticated, risky projects, and your most mature and courageous supporters.

Obviously you don't ask a national funder to support the local fun run, or ask the local or branch bank to fund your partnership with three other urban museums across the country addressing the role of public protest in political change. You could, however, ask the local or branch bank to fund the fun run or a local presentation and discussion that is part of the partnership on public protest in political change. And you could ask the regional arm of a national funder to help support that same partnership when it has a much broader reach. If you have a local arts council, then it is appropriate to apply for support for a stand-alone presentation or workshop, or to apply for partial support of the entire fall series. If the series goes to multiple towns, you may be able to apply to multiple arts councils to support it as it comes to their community. Another approach is to leverage a series' longer-running and higher profile into a request to a regional funder or business. Since the larger scale offers any funder more opportunities to connect with the public, the regional bank may find this project more attractive than a single-town lecture. The request amount increases with the breadth of the project reach.

Sometimes a project is likely to be a long one, taking place over years. For this type, you must map the funders along with the anticipated project growth so that you can ask for the right amount of money

The How Family Home, Burlington County Historical Society, New Jersey
Courtesy of Burlington County Historical Society

from the funders who are most closely aligned with the project at each stage. Here's an example: The Burlington County Historical Society (BCHS) is becoming a children's history experience. It has two distinct exhibit spaces for these young explorers—the How House and the Corson Poley Center. The How House is a historic structure; the Corson Poley Center is a modern, open shell with flexible space for exhibits and programming. The staff and their consultants are steadily doing the exhibit research, design, and protoyping to create the Children's History Center across these spaces. This is a small organization with a big goal. The state funding agency had been very supportive, but the annual requests to the state for operating and project funds cannot satisfy all the institutional needs. So after receving a few state grants for initial planning and then initial design for the exhibits in the How House and Corson Poley Center, BCHS needed to broaden its funder circle to fund more collections research to support the exhibit. IMLS was an obvious target for collections management and documentation work, but BCHS had never applied before. The entry-level tier, $25,000 with no match required, seemed like the place to try. The application was successful! The next year BCHS applied for planning and prototyping group programs in the How House at the same level. That grant was unsuccessful, but the reviewer comments were so positive that the staff felt a second, improved application the next year was appropriate. The second application was successful. When the work was complete, BCHS followed up with a second proposal to expand the practice to designing prototyping exhibits for school group audiences, supported by the new questions and answers developed during the previous grant.

When BCHS launches the effort to install the exhibit in the Corson Poley Center, it will be time to apply for a multiyear IMLS grant program to fund the nonconstruction aspects of finalizing and implementing the new exhibit. That will also be the perfect time to ask all local funders to pitch in on the project. BCHS is likely to attract the support of local foundations more easily and can begin creating a continuing grants program to keep the exhibit active and refreshed. Then future major grants from agencies such as IMLS can fund expanded programming and more opportunities to research child learning and to extend the impact through traveling modules designed to

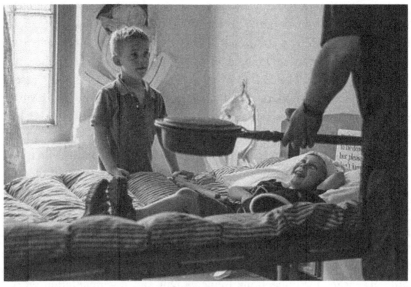

History Isn't Boring at How House!
Courtesy of Burlington County Historical Society

be adapted to each locale, and by developing professional training programs for peers.

This timeline is currently dominated by agency funding: state and federal. This type of funding focuses on quality and effectiveness of museum practice, which, once at full steam, will be the foundation for future local impact. That means that the local funding will follow agency funding for this organization, which is unusual. Take care to be open to creating a strategy that suits your organization and the projects at hand, not someone else's formula for success. If BCHS had waited, it would never have been able to begin such an important project.

Sometimes you do not anticipate the actual growth and success of the program, so you do not map the sequence of funders and the tiers of funding from the beginning. Just adjust your targets as you discover the increased value. When the project is so successful that you partner with others to implement it across more locations or audiences, or on a larger scale, then you will notice the project aligning with the next tier of funders, and you will make the adjustments.

Institutional Goals

Tiers in funding and projects apply to the evolution of organizations as well as projects and programs. As a new organization, your targets will be Tier I: smaller, more local, requiring—and funding—less complex projects. You can move up based on your grant successes. Initially, you may have no Tier III, and likely no Tier IV grants on your list, but as you gain a couple of years of grant experience, your plan should begin to consider a long-range goal of a Tier III grant in five years or more, and a Tier IV in eight or more. Few organizations will be able to attract national grants for the scale and reach of their program, but they may be able to attract them for the quality of the project and the strategic approach in their work.

A good credibility-building process is the Standards and Excellence Program for Historical Institutions (StEPs), a self-assessment program created and managed by the American Association for State and Local History (AASLH) with the support of IMLS grants. The set-your-own pace program allows you to explore roadmaps to improving institutional performance in six categories: mission, vision, and governance; audience;

interpretation; stewardship of collections; stewardship of historic structures and landscapes; and management. There are training modules and worksheets to help your institution proceed through the sections, earning certificates as you go. These certificates are recognized as fulfillment of peer-reviewed standards or excellence. They will encourage a funder that you know what you are doing and you are worth the support.

An excellent way to jump from very local funders to something with more name recognition is to pursue grants tied closely to the profession. This includes preservation grants from the National Trust for Historic Preservation, Collections Assessment for Preservation (CAP) awards through the Foundation for the American Institute of Conservation of Historic and Artistic Works (FAIC), Museum Assessment Program (MAP) grants from IMLS, and Preservation Assistance Grants (PAG) from the National Endowment for the Humanities. They are designed for smaller organizations or smaller projects, often at museums that have not received support from these agencies. They are gateways to larger grants. These awards confer credibility on the awardee, and your successful completion labels you as performing to shared preservation or management standards. This supports *their* mission, too. Remember, these funders want to give you money; they *want* you to come to them with a good or great program. Their own tiered process will help your organization develop professionally and strengthen your credibility with the agency when you apply for larger grants. These awards also encourage other funders by assuring them of your basic credentials and reducing their perceived risks in supporting you.

Here's a tiered plan for a hypothetical small industrial museum on the edge of an urban area, with a strong suburban audience:

What Tier I Looks Like

- You apply to bank branches and arts councils in two or three of the nearby towns or counties for a series of local summer presentations on "How did our town get built this way?" The programs will take place in any community where you can find funding for a presentation.
- You submit applications to the three private foundations you are pretty sure will say "yes," and ask for support of an educator to

design and deliver classroom programs related to "How did our town get built this way?" You spread the programs as far as the money allows you to. You plan to do this each year to support your exhibits and constantly upgrade the programs' delivery or reach (or both).

- For the first time, you submit an NEH Preservation grant for re-housing and inventorying the recent gift of 350 items. They were collected by an engineer who had worked at the missile plant during each of the three corporate ownerships over the past forty-five years. The records will be part of the next summer's talks on "Working History in the Cold River Area." This processing must be done somehow. With a grant, the housing materials will be new and special ordered, and you can fund a contractual scholar to complete the work in a few months. Without funding, you will have to scavenge housing materials and supervise an intern or volunteer(s) to process the collection over twelve to eighteen months. You realize that if you don't get the grant, you could also consider reapplying next year using the reviewer comments to strengthen the proposal. You could substitute a different program for next summer's talks that requires less new processing and research.
- You plan to use StEPs to help you assess your institution's performance and identify priority needs. You choose the Stewardship of Collections category first so you can use your more thorough understanding of your collections and collections processes to attract a MAP II (Museum Assessment Program for Collections) or CAP (Collections Assessment for Preservation) grant to follow. You plan to choose the MAP III Audience Engagement category next year or eighteen months from now to help you make the case for program funding through local foundations.

What Tier II Looks Like

- You have a string of successful local branch and arts council applications and are now trying to alternate years or projects. Make sure to talk with the managers to see what interests them most now. You want to keep them engaged, give them exposure, but not overuse them.

- Your private foundations list is expanding to include more targets, the requests are larger, and the response rate is stronger. You plan to add a couple new Tier I funders to your active list each year if the pool will bear it. Be sure to continue to cultivate existing funders as they move to Tier II even as you add new ones.
- You've completed a few of the StEPs sections, you are trying to fit in a CAP or MAP application. You decide which is the most important—CAP for conservation, or MAP for I (Administration), II, III, or IV (Governance). You will identify which one supports the needs identified in the strategic plan, or the one you need the most, and use the recommendations to make your case for future support from grantors. You plan to choose one this year and one each of the next four years until you work through them all.
- Consider the IMLS $25,000 no-match grant to complete processing your collection. Be sure to explain how that grant dramatically simplifies exhibit and programming research by improving intellectual access to the collection and gives you an opportunity to connect your collection to others around the country for online research and potential loan opportunities. Industry is changing so rapidly that we must be sure to document the past even as we are collecting and documenting the present.
- Consider, if you've done a CAP grant on your collection, whether it is appropriate now to do one for the building(s). Be sure not to do all the assessments so close together that you cannot raise the funds or fit in all the work identified; space them out to spread the work, but do start with the most urgent needs.
- Can you find a cooperative project where you and another organization each apply for funding? Practicing cooperation on a small, safe scale will improve your institutional knowledge and prepare you for more complex projects and funding later on. You can use the successes here in future proposals to demonstrate experience in collaboration.
- Consider whether it's time to apply to the state for support of preservation, research, or programming. You may have a preservation project to fund or a statewide celebration to support. Or perhaps the state funds preservation and you have an old mill structure that needs an engineering review after all these years. This is a safe

way to start a funding relationship with the state while paying for an assessment that will give you a third-party description of your capital repair needs for future grant requests.

What Tier III Looks Like

- You've left behind the smallest local grant requests and taken a seat on the arts council board.
- Your private foundation funders now sometimes contact you with an automatic gift for the coming year, saying that while they are doing some internal planning and assessment they are continuing funding for existing grantees to the same or similar programming.
- You now plan to skip an application year with funders if you don't have a new project to bring them, giving them a rest and spending your energy on cultivating new funders.
- Over the last few years you have worked through the entry-point applications to NEH, IMLS, and the National Trust. You no longer qualify for those, so you focus on the larger, multiyear applications.

What Tier IV Looks Like

- There are many community infrastructure needs that you can be a part of, such as open spaces, improved transportation, public gathering spaces, and natural resource management. You'll be doing good work of your own while supporting a state initiative.
- You apply for the more specialized national grants from each agency, and for new program grants as they come along.
- You realize that you earn those national grants almost every time you apply; you begin to apply for collaborations (local, regional, or national) where what you learn can be shared broadly for the benefit of many organizations.

As you get further into your grant experience, you will notice that even as you reach the point where you have matured to working at Tier III or IV, new projects and programs, and new funders, are likely to fit better in Tiers I or II. This is a fluid system; expect to move around within it.

All the assessment opportunities may seem overwhelming, but they are worth pursuing when they support your strategic needs. Patiently working through them will strengthen your funding future, as will using entry-level grants before major proposals. You may have to stagger these, so, again, even though you reach Tier III funding in some aspects, others may just be getting started at the Tier I level. A well-developed program will have projects and funders progressing through the tiers year to year.

Dumbarton House, Headquarters for the National Society of the Colonial Dames of America

Dumbarton House is a great example of how to grow a grants program and how to progress through tiers of funding. The program started with a few gifts from new area foundation donors, and grants targeted to support professional practice in historic preservation and collections care. The team became better at identifying and articulating its role in addition to traditional house museum practice, and at articulating its impact among broader audiences. With coaching from funders, Dumbarton House created an advisory board that allowed the institu-

"Before" image for window restoration at Dumbarton House as part of the NEH Sustaining Cultural Heritage Collections project
Courtesy of Dumbarton House/National Society of the Colonial Dames of America, Washington, D.C.

tion to expand and diversify its leadership while adhering to the legal requirements of lineage-based board membership criteria. All along, the strong practice of engaging the board in all the organization's work made it much easier to earn its support for new approaches, particularly environmental sustainability, which opened new sources of funding for serious capital projects and propelled the institution to Tier III funders and projects. Over five years it developed to a point where Dumbarton House earned a six-figure implementation grant from the National Endowment for the Humanities.

At a different organization, the indicators for reaching Tier III were a grant from the major urban community foundation, a grant from the state, and a grant from the National Science Foundation. The powerful local support, the statewide recognition, and the national recognition were seals of approval that have since sustained funding at an impressive level. Reaching that level took five years of steady cultivation of local funders to build and expand programs, and to develop the infrastructure to dependably deliver quality programs and articulate their impact. It meant acquiring the equipment for programs, software for evaluation, a track record for audience reach, and a steadily growing list of weighty endorsements in the form of local foundations. The

"After" image for window restoration at Dumbarton House as part of the NEH Sustaining Cultural Heritage Collections project
Courtesy of Dumbarton House/National Society of the Colonial Dames of America, Washington, D.C.

staff was diligent in cultivating relationships with funders by inviting them to events to see the site and meet participants, and by meeting with the funder before applications whenever possible. Along the way, the organization kept a grant income goal in its budget that was a slight stretch but was adapted as the year went on. Some proposals were unsuccessful that first year but became proven income sources in subsequent years.

WHEN IS THE RIGHT TIME TO START A GRANTS PROGRAM?

The right time to start a grants program is as soon as you complete this book. Once you finish reading, here's how to proceed. First, consider, as you assess the organization in the next chapter, preparing policies and identifying targets and projects to be the beginning of your program. Once you've done that, you can partner with a more experienced agency, start with very small grants on your own, or apply for an assessment grant to demonstrate your needs as you begin applying for expanded support. We've discussed assessment grants; let's look at partner and solo grants.

Partnering

One valuable strategy for a new grants program is to ride the coattails of other organizations more experienced in raising grant money. When the lead institution applies for support, then you, as a partner in the project, gain exposure to the funder and the benefits of increased impact through collaboration. If the application and project are successful, you can tell other funders that you participated in a project funded by the Mercury Foundation. It's the first step in building your funding credibility.

Your First Solo Applications

If you're new to grant fundraising and you don't have a more experienced partner to work with, the first step is to establish credibility by completing a project, then by funding it externally. That means that you will have to self-fund your projects and programs with earned income, annual appeals, or special and in-kind gifts, plus sheer creativity. This track record builds your organization's résumé, proving that you have the planning ability, public interest, and performance record worthy of foundation support. As you transition those ideas and projects from internal funding to grant funding, you can incubate new ideas and make room for more projects while continuing these and building your grants reputation. By beginning with reasonable expectations and modest requests for modest projects, you can efficiently build your fundraising track record until you can command bigger gifts for more significant projects.

Be ready: All organizations suffer through letters that begin with "We're sorry to inform you" or "Thank you for applying. It was a very competitive round this time . . ." We all live through it. When you focus on the annual deadlines, this process seems excruciatingly slow, but quickly you will find yourself at that deadline a second and third time—with the corresponding years of experience behind you and your institution. By combining persistence with a willingness to learn from the process, success will come. A few easy "wins" can make all the difference as you go solo. So, apply to the local arts or humanities council even if the award is only a few hundred dollars. Ask the banks for support, and ask a friend's business to sponsor something. Next year you can ask for a bit more money, and you can apply to more funders on the strength of last year's record.

As you make your first applications, remember to assess other important benefits to applying. Sometimes it is worth making the application for a small amount of money simply because you need that donor's name on your support list. There are benefits from the process as well. It helps you:

- begin a relationship with the funder
- place your materials before its board members and thereby expand your circle of acquaintance
- force yourself to practice the process and collect or update the necessary proposal materials
- acquire feedback about your proposal

At all times in your grant efforts, and especially at the beginning, it is critical that you triage your efforts for efficiency. The record-keeping and case-making aspects that support the grants process are practices you employ as you manage your museum, but sometimes formatting and writing it up as a proposal requires more effort than the cash award will truly be worth. After you factor in staff time, preparing the proposal, and collecting supporting materials, it may not make sense to keep applying for $1,000 or $2,000 or even $5,000 because you may not get the grant, it may be awarded at a lower amount, or the maximum award may not be enough money to really help you move forward.

If much of the effort is already spent because the application has already been written once for another funder, then the investment in editing that information for these small grants becomes much more proportionate to the return. For example, if you're already going to apply to one foundation for $10,000, then applying to the Waialua Arts Council for its ceiling amount of $2,500 becomes more palatable than if the council were your only target. The proposal can't be copied verbatim because each funder is so different, but there are economies of effort when you can reuse a concept and information in subsequent proposals to support the same project.

You must determine your own threshold of effort, combined with potential for income and the size of that potential income, to make your decision. You will have to choose among these costs each time you consider an application. Be sure the staff and board understand this threshold concept and the risks involved so that disappointments and disagreements do not derail an otherwise thoughtful process. Then make notes in the funder file about why you chose to apply. You'll appreciate them when you get the response and when you consider the next application to that donor.

CONCLUSION

Looking back, years from now, your grants program trajectory will likely mirror the first three stages; some institutions will reach the fourth stage.

- Early period: Apply for only Tier I grants, gradually increasing in size and expanding in reach. You keep track of them on a computer spreadsheet.
- Middle period: Applying for Tier I and II grants has created a steady base of funders, with a few annual additions based on new or expanded programming or projects. You'll notice funders approaching you. You've invested in donor management software, or expanded what you have to include the management of institutional donors.
- Mature period: Now your grants come from three tiers. There's a very solid base of supporters with annual additions plus some higher-profile, more complex projects moving program performance and nonfixed capital assets to a whole new level. Sometimes funders call on you for special projects or introduce you to other potential funding partners.
- Stretch period: This is much like your "Mature" period, but you may pursue some fixed capital projects such as major renovations and expansions, or major new exhibits or high-profile collaborations that open new audiences and new focus areas. You may apply to Tier IV funders.

Naturally, institutions sometimes move backward on this schedule as well. The key is to consider the whole process of pursuing grants as a critical program at your institution rather than as an emergency or stopgap measure. Now let's look at how to get your institution really ready to support all this good research and planning.

NOTES

1. "The Sector's Economic Impact," Independent Sector, accessed September 22, 2016, https://www.independentsector.org/economic_role.

2. The comments in this section were derived from comments by Sally Zinno in the 2005 edition of *Is Your Museum Grant-Ready?*

CHAPTER 4

Is Your Museum Grant-Ready?

It's a terrific moment when your organization crosses that threshold between "good" and "fundable." You will feel it one day as a number of successes coincide: the annual appeal surpasses its goal, your attendance grows well for the second year running, and the flagship education program attracts a community service award. That is when you move from asking only friends and family for gifts to approaching other institutions—foundations and government agencies. Whether you are really "there," though, is something too few institutions have thoughtfully considered.

Yes, you have probably evaluated yourself based on the field standards—mission, management, programs—but remember, the field will not be funding you. Grant readiness is a measure of institutional effectiveness in terms *the funder* values. Foundation officers ask themselves: Does this museum do something we believe in, in a manner we can endorse, that makes effective use of resources for significant, needed change? And does it behave in a way that encourages us to be associated with it? Here is what you can ask yourself from a foundation's point of view:

- Do you do something important?
- For anyone in particular?
- Do you do it well?
- Do you make a difference?
- Are you a smart investment?
- Are you a good partner?

- What's your edge?
- Will they want to work with you again?

Since proposals are turned down for a myriad of reasons outside the control of the applicant, keep in mind that you cannot anticipate those barriers to your success: there may be a change in donor interest, a torrent of crisis-based proposals that appeal to the funder at that moment in time, or perhaps too many similar proposals from better-known organizations that time around. Still, you *can* identify your own barriers and remove them. That's the grant-readiness process and the reason why it is important to assess the institution's readiness to apply for grants. This self-audit educates both the staff and the board about the common expectations of funders, the performance requirements on your part, and reasonable hopes for success. Understandably, the growth and maturation of an organization has a great deal to do with grant readiness, and maturation is a long process, but understanding what readiness is and working toward it as your organization matures will help you become fundable faster.

The grant-ready checklist is a shorthand way to organize your thinking as you work through articulating your institution's ability to attract grants. Chances are that your organization has many of the components it needs to convince the funder that you are ready, or nearly so. Your job is to learn what readiness looks like, and then achieve and maintain it at your institution even as the competition gets harder. You may discover through this assessment that you need to bring some components up to speed before beginning applications. Maybe you will find that simply documenting what you do, the need for it, and its quality will be enough to get you ready. Better yet, when you're done with this book, perhaps you will confirm your readiness and can confidently commit resources to a grants program.

DO YOU DO SOMETHING IMPORTANT?

What do you do, and why does it matter? You must be able to explain how the work makes a difference and why you are best suited to do this work, and you must explain how you fulfill needs that are documented rather than merely perceived.

GRANT-READY CHECKLIST

Do You Do Something Important?
Can you show the need?
Are you the only one doing this? Why or why not?

For Anyone in Particular?
Can you describe your audience?
Why this particular audience?
Are there others you may serve in the future?

Do You Do It Well?
Do you make a difference?
   Can you show your impact as significant and appropriate?
   Can you describe your work in terms of *benefits*, not *features*?
Can you demonstrate the quality of your personnel and operations?
   Do you have qualified consultants, collaborators, advisors, staff, board
      members, and volunteers?
   Are you accredited or qualified in appropriate ways?
Do you demonstrate programmatic success?
   Do you evaluate your programs?
   Do you continue to improve your performance?

Are You a Smart Investment?
Are your management practices clear and sound?
   Are your governing documents appropriate and up to date?
   Are your policies and procedures complete?
   Do you have and use appropriate operating or strategic plans?
How about financial management?
   Is your financial situation reasonable?
   Do you review your financial condition regularly?
   Are there guidelines for managing gifts, grants, and investments?

Are You a Good Partner?
Internally?
   Do you apply your mission internally?
   Did you manage the project intelligently and well?
   Did you say "thank you" for grants? More than once?
   Do you nurture the relationship?

(continued)

GRANT-READY CHECKLIST *(continued)*

Externally?
    Do you consider the external situation when making decisions?
    Can you show how you contribute to the community?
    Can you demonstrate successful, credible partnerships?

What's Your Edge?
Do you maximize the donor's impact by replicating or extending the project?
Do you have a professional or innovative edge to distinguish you?

Will They Want to Work with You Again?
Would you want to work with you?

Can You Show the Need?

How do you explain that you're doing something that matters? If it is important, there must be a visible need for this project or work. Look for evidence based on the source of the need: it may be internally generated, audience generated, or community generated. Is it important to address this so that you can fulfill your mission? Has your audience expressed a need or interest? Or have you seen it in the community and are responding? It's critical that you document it clearly with evidence as statistics or as third-party requests, preferably both. The sources should be highly reliable print and online articles, government statistics, public feedback, or the research of think tanks or foundations.

Internal needs are those that address your physical site, your institutional resources, and your institution's ability to do its job:

- Do your evaluations demonstrate an interest in programming for which your staff needs more professional development, such as serving autistic children or presenting socially charged topics?
- Did you have a preservation or conservation assessment done that indicates the extent of professional attention required and the sequence of which projects to take on first?

- Did you review your investment policy and determine your wish to increase your socially responsible holdings but need special advice to do so?
- Did you move the new parking lot up higher on the capital projects list? Was it because so many parents bringing their kids to your children's museum—in strollers—complained about the potholes and uneven surface of the current one?

Some needs arise in the community, and you intend to address them in the ways that align with your mission:

- Did the prison outreach program request a preservation skills workshop?
- In the exit survey from the last exhibit, did visitors ask specifically for a new topic or approach?
- Do teachers' requests or the visitor log demonstrate a specific need or interest area?
- Does the frequency of historic home demolition in your area indicate a lack of awareness on the benefits of historic preservation?
- Is your city or town seeing a growing number of immigrants? Is there a need for programming that provides a historical overview and present-day information to ease newcomers' transitions and engage the community in the benefits of this diversity?
- Does a recent increase in homelessness make your historic settlement house site a critical venue for public awareness and neighborhood planning?

In the 1990s, when many states implemented curriculum frameworks, guidelines, or standards, for the first time in each school grade the requirements gave historical organizations ready-made needs statements for programming by grade level. When museums wanted to make the case for funding so the programs could be offered for free, the school district statistics on underserved groups backed up the case. As states continue to establish and update curriculum guidelines, you have a ready-made case for requesting support to create or renew your programs and promote those offerings to a large audience.

Are You the Only One Doing This? Why or Why Not?

Still, you need more than a request or even a demonstrated need to convince the funder that this is important. You must prove that the need is currently unmet, that you fill a gap left by the others around you, and that no one else is solving this problem (or, perhaps, addressing it the way you do). Be careful here, though. Every applicant will tell the funder that it is "unique," but how many unique approaches can there truly be? Strive instead for "distinctive." Simply be clear on how you are distinct from other approaches in particular ways. To make this case, you must first know what is being done, or not done, around you: you must know your market comparables. The first level of comparison is institutional:

- What are the other historic homes associated with authors or artists, presidents, or other statesmen?
- Are there other special-interest technology museums you should know about?
- Is there another state, local, or regional group covering your home territory? How large are their budgets and facilities?

The next level is program delivery:

- What are their offerings; who are their partners and their audiences?
- What is their attendance and their programming by comparison?
- Do the other gardens or nature centers have similar programs, or is there a gap you fill?
- Is anyone else solving the problem in the way you do? If no, that would help make your point.

Once you identify these distinctions, then make the case for why you work in this area in this manner, but without focusing on how others are somehow going about this all wrong. Instead, explain how your choices align with your mission, strategic commitments, institutional assets, and audience needs. In the process, you will identify your organization and its work as the most appropriate to fill this need, and you will demonstrate how thoughtful you were in designing the program to address this need now and in this way.

DO YOU DO THIS FOR ANYONE IN PARTICULAR?

"Need" is an audience-dependent concept, so the funder, to be sure its grant funds reach the intended audience, will want to know who benefits from your work. This means you'll be describing the people and organizations you have in your audience, or the new ones you are trying to reach. The challenge is that the funder may describe audiences in ways that are very different from how the audiences see themselves, or how you see the audiences. Each approach is valid; your responsibility is to determine which descriptions to use for soliciting information from users and for sharing audience descriptions with the funder.

Can You Describe Your Audience?

For example, the funder's categories on its website and online proposal cover sheet may be "socially excluded," "with limited access to cultural resources," and "underserved." These labels may be quite different from how you identify visitors and how they identify themselves. Your categories may be children without after-school care, families, festival guests, students enrolled in English as a Second Language, high school students, or immigrants. Your visitors likely describe themselves more concretely, based on geographical residence, profession, museum interest, and age and social unit. You will use all of these descriptions in your work, whether to define an audience or to tailor your work to serve them. So, let's look at how you might describe your audience.

First, identify your current users by:

- tracking demographics at point-of-sale with zip code and source information
- using sign-in sheets indicating origin by town, program, or state
- taking periodic user surveys at your website or in the museum
- monitoring community demographics and their changes

Second, group your current audiences by interactions:

- walk-in visitors
- groups (school or tours) with name or source

- special events guests
- age (at least to the level of child, youth, adult, and senior)
- grouping (family, meet-up)
- ethnicity (not by verbal questioning or visual guessing but if they define themselves accordingly in a survey they complete, or if the group they are traveling with provides this information)
- frequency of visits and whether this is the first visit (for the group or the individual, accordingly)

Third, uncover motivation and decision making:

- how they heard about you and why they came to visit
- if a particular event or exhibit enticed them for this visit
- if a student needed information for further study
- if they have family or other guests with them

The goal is to trap as much information as possible without burdening the visitor. Be sure to explain that this information helps you make your case to donors who help fund your programs and facilities. Tailor your queries to those categories that make the most sense for your work, but imagine, as widely as possible, the types of information your funders will want to see. If you collect anecdotal feedback, someone on the front line should take note of personal conversations with your audience that by accident, or design, tell you about their needs and interests. Those encounters and quotes are very valuable when it comes time to write the proposal. You may have to observe and speak with visitors yourself to get these, but they are worth the time, as they make proposal writing so much easier and effective. However you choose to proceed, you will end up with multiple categories for describing your audiences—theirs, yours, and the funders'—and each has value in describing the reasons behind your work.

Since you cannot collect information from every visitor, and you likely are hoping to reach new populations, the U.S. Census can help you describe the broader audience pool available to you. The free online datasets have a great deal of information about the residents of the counties and states you serve. The datasets contain concrete details about population size and historical and expected loss or growth;

veteran status, age, sex, race, ancestry, Hispanic origin, and migration; and language use. So, when you say that you are targeting a veteran audience, the census can provide that information. This can help you describe your potential group of participants or demonstrate the lack of diversity in your area and the need to provide mobile formats of exhibits and programs so that you can reach a more diverse audience. It's all there, free of charge, but you have to go into the databases and explore them to discover what they can offer you.

Why This Particular Audience?

Make sure to explain why this audience is the one you have chosen to serve. First of all, does the audience need to align with your mission? Sometimes it's obvious, and sometimes you have to make a clearer connection. The immediate audiences might look like these:

- Your rural community has no other cultural resources than the local library. As a historical museum, you feel a responsibility to reach those who might have limited access to cultural programming because they do not travel to nearby cities or do not travel for work or vacation consistently. You believe that cultural access should not be limited to those who can afford travel.
- You are an arts organization, and the community just lost municipal funding for arts in the schools, or the local mental health agency has no art therapy program. You would like to offer what is needed, and you have the skilled staff and collections resources to support that programming.
- You are a science and nature center, and you have determined that the local extension service has been looking for a place for projects pairing master naturalists and 4-H clubs for cooperative learning. Your studies and programs in your re-created prairie and native grasses test beds are perfect settings for engaging learners of every age.

Here are some examples of working with an audience that may seem surprising to the funder. What might seem like a stretch at first is justified with data.

- As an art museum, many of your paintings and photographs contain visual details that are a test for the viewer. Perhaps you wish to support community police in building their observation skills and human understanding by providing tours with a trained consultant.[1] You will need to document the success of similar programs and then relate your design to theirs; then demonstrate, likely through a letter from, or agreement with, the police department, that the intended audience is interested. Do not forget to explain why you are the one local arts agency appropriate for this work. Perhaps you've had previous experience in this program, or your security personnel can add valuable perspective, or you have the most appropriate art for this kind of programming. Abstract art just would not do.
- As a history museum, you have interpreted the waves of immigrant history to your community in the past. Do your lawmakers and enforcers, and your community members, recognize the historical patterns and parallels with the most recent wave of immigrants? Do you know the newest immigrants as well as you think you know them? Can the community benefit from your support for a more integrated telling of these stories? By illustrating the demographic changes using census data and referencing the professional shift from talking about someone as "other" to inviting them to contribute to conversations, you can make a case for reaching out to all these audiences in new ways in support of mission-supportive research and programming.

What about Future Audiences?

Just as you can place funders in sequential tiers and approach them, your program matures, and you may have a list of future audience groups you wish to reach as your programs or capacity develop. If a funder is interested in an audience you do not serve yet but one you legitimately hope to serve in the future, or is interested in an audience you hope to grow significantly, it is reasonable to ask for support to prepare to serve that audience. As an example, as the Burlington County Historical Society develops its Children's History Museum, it is working to reach expanded family audiences. Doing so requires the design and installation of exhibits for the reimagined space and the adjacent historic house and testing of exhibit elements to ensure their effectiveness. Grant funding from the New Jersey Council on the Arts, and from IMLS, was based on the demonstration of the lack of such opportunities in the area, the soundness of the research into the effectiveness of children's history programs, and institutional planning affirming this as the society's mission. In the design phase the project does not yet serve that audience, but all evidence indicates that it will when the planning is complete, so this proposal supports future audiences that the funder values.

Now, how do you convince the funder that you will be able to achieve that future goal? By demonstrating that you have the talent and experience and resources to do this work well.

DO YOU DO IT WELL?

If your work matters, don't you want to make a difference, do the work well, and continue to improve upon your work? These concepts are related, and they have greater impact if you describe them clearly in your proposal.

Do You Make a Difference?

A difference is a change: in people it can be a change in awareness, knowledge, and understanding; in people or an institution it can be a change in ability and capacity, or a change in behavior. For example, you may be really good at costume conservation. Terrific! Make sure the funder understands that is what you *do*, but when your work also protects materials from long-term damage, makes them available for public exhibit, or provides information valuable to historical or costume research, you are making a *difference* in your institution's ability to care for and display its collection and to conduct programs that raise awareness, provide knowledge, and improve understanding. Perhaps an exhibit on clothing choices can change people's choices when it comes to purchasing more environmentally—and socially—responsible clothing. Remember to explain that *difference*, not just what you *do*, to the funder.

Can You Show Your Impact as Significant and Appropriate?

Remember, the impact to emphasize is the impact relevant to the funder. A historic preservation funder is interested in building- and site-related impacts, particularly, so the clothing exhibit and the conservation that contributes to it will not be of interest. If you are a house museum and there are fifteen thousand of them in the United States, what difference does yours make for its audience? In its successful application to the 1772 Foundation for a maintenance assessment of a historic structure, the Burlington County Historical Society had to make the case for the Bard How House in a way appropriate to the scale of a historic home and to the interests of a preservation funder. This is the section of the fill-in form for that application:

The difference this house makes: During 2015–2016 the BCHS staff worked with an educational consultant funded by a grant from the Institute of Museum & Library Services to develop goals and outcomes, and to pilot new activities at How House to strengthen its visitor engagement. The big challenge is to help visitors think of How House as a historic house where touching is encouraged, even expected! We wanted to create the visual and spatial clues that encourage visitors of all ages to explore the house in a hands-on way. We determined that improved lighting, contextual images, interpretive text, and wayfinding tools can help visitors understand the kinds of activities they can do in the house. These and other design changes create a different feel to the space, one that communicates that the How House is not a traditional historic house museum but rather a kids' space and completely hands-on. Now we have applied for support for the consultant to help us design school visits by working with Burlington teachers to create a program supporting curriculum requirements while encouraging self-directed learning by schools. This immersive approach provokes creative play and generates cognitive and social benefits for students and their teachers.

The result is that we have an extremely accessible historic house where children and their families, students and their teachers, can connect with a historic property and the story of the people who once lived there. Our goal is to build fun and engaging connections with history that builds lifelong fans of history and historic places. This is the public part of preservation work that creates supporters of historic properties in the future.

Can You Describe Your Work in Terms of Benefits *and* Features?

A trick for doing this is to look at your work in terms of *benefits*, not only *features*. The features are the activities, or the products, or the processes; the benefits are the discoveries, opportunities, and changes that have lasting value in support of your mission. Table 4.1 has examples.

Table 4.1. Features and Benefits
These three examples are for very different types of projects. Each illustrates how explaining the difference, rather than simply describing the features, makes for a clearer and much more compelling case.

Features	Benefits!
Conserve ten dresses worn by Mrs. Madelaine Johansen and her daughters in the 1920s.	Conservators get a rare look at reuse of materials and dress construction while conserving flour sack dresses. This provides an opportunity to create accurate historical patterns for site interpreters and, as a bonus, makes them for sale in the gift shop.
Renovate the courtyard, main entrance, and parking lot using native plantings, engineering a permeable surface and a water catchment system, creating a handicapped accessible front door that is an easy-to-recognize entrance.	This proposal will address problems of visitor confusion about which entrance to use by making it attractive and inviting; improve handicapped accessibility for all visitors, eliminating the need to send wheelchairs to the side door; and improve parking for visitors of all abilities while also addressing stormwater runoff issues to improve local water quality, reduce community infrastructure needs, and save the museum money.
Offer a new arts and creativity program during after-school hours for local children ages 9–13 (the museum is located one block from the school).	The proximity of the museum to the school means that local families can enroll children for the time in between the end of the school day and when parents can get home from work, without needing to provide transportation. The program is an important alternative for students uninterested in the sports and music programs available at the school during that time.

Sometimes the funder helps make their interest clear in this by wording the question in a way that encourages you to describe benefits. For the National Endowment for the Humanities' Preservation Assistance Grants, where nearly everyone is requesting materials and supplies or consulting time, the differentiation comes out in the question on the effects on the institution. This is another example of a successful proposal from the Burlington County Historical Society:

What is the importance of this project to the institution?

The proposed Collection Assessment and Preservation Plan will be a fundamental component of institutional planning. The Plan will establish preservation needs of the collection as BCHS considers capital projects, and guide staff as they incorporate collections care and management into strategic planning. For example, the project will introduce professional standards to the process of converting a small, BCHS-owned office building for collections processing and storage if it is recommended.

BCHS staff recognizes the need to establish a proper standard of care, and physical and intellectual control over the collections. Collections are generally located in secure, nonpublic storage areas, placed on modular storage equipment, and housed in acid-free containers. Environmental monitoring routines need to be improved. Some areas are overcrowded, and use of space could be improved. Collections prep and handling areas are not conveniently located.

The Preservation Plan will identify priorities including space use and storage planning; design of housing systems for collections; conservation treatment priorities for collections; modifications to collections policies and procedures; training needs for staff; and improvements to environmental monitoring systems and controls. The plan will also include a list of potential funding sources supporting preservation activities, and provide a recommended sequence of work to address the scope of the plan.

This work addresses a gap identified in the 2010 Master Plan. It will identify specific needs for strengthening ongoing care for the collections and raise awareness among staff and trustees in a manner that highlights priorities and assists with fundraising for collections care. With the involvement of a highly qualified conservator, this plan will reflect current professional standards of collections care and provide sound and reasonable strategies for the preservation and management of the collection. Through this project BCHS will accrue other benefits:

- Staff will establish an ongoing relationship with an outside conservator who is knowledgeable about all aspects of collections care and is available for future initiatives, such as refurbishing the office building and relocating all or portions of collection storage.
- The Project Conservator will become familiar with the organization and therefore be better prepared to serve as a future resource for counsel and advice.
- During the Assessment experience, the project team will be able to evaluate existing procedures and identify immediate improvements to collection care activities.

This project comes at a time when staff will soon be able to lift their heads from the work of shepherding the new Children's History Center exhibit design and installation and can turn to collections management work that supports the institutional mission for care and preservation and the future evolution of the Children's History Center exhibit materials and themes.

DO YOU DO IT IN A WAY THAT MATTERS?

The next step is to explain why the difference matters. Here are ideas for some of the examples in table 4.1:

- For the costume restoration and programming example, perhaps it matters because you are trying to differentiate yourself from area attractions based on authenticity, and documentation for historically correct costumes is an important way to do that.
- For a construction project, if you have evidence of visitor complaints or confusion about your entrance, and if there is documentation of the changes in sewerage costs for stormwater issues in your community, then you can demonstrate how, through the elements of the new design, your project will make the desired difference.
- For creativity programming, use national research to make the case for creativity and art among other offerings of music and sports; then identify the number of two-income households in your area and the need for more safe and valuable out-of-school activities for children. Highlight the uniqueness of being able to use a museum-orchestrated "walking-bus" approach to transport the children from school to the museum, where they are later collected by their parents.

Can You Demonstrate the Quality of Your Personnel and Operations?

By illustrating the quality of your personnel and operations, you are reassuring the funder that your institution has the professional resources to design and deliver good projects and good work. If there are no areas of concern, you need not address all these issues specifically, but if there is anything that could affect the grant or reflect badly on you, then take the time and text to be preemptive and address those concerns. Your goal is to quiet every question in the reader's mind so that he or she is willing to commit to you. Let's start with personnel.

Do You Have Qualified Consultants, Collaborators,
Advisors, Staff, and Volunteers?

Do your staff and volunteers have the education, training, talent, and resources appropriate for this institution and where it is headed? One reason many funders ask for an organizational chart, if they do, is to help sort out some of these issues quickly. Be sure to convince the reviewers that you have the right staff in position and that they have the authority to do their job. If your staff is not qualified for some aspects of the work or not large enough to complete the work, then do you have a plan to help them acquire those skills, or to collaborate with and learn from others who do? You may have consultants and volunteers to help with the work. You do not have to describe every staff member, consultant, or volunteer, just those integral to the project and as space allows.

Do your volunteers do meaningful work, in appropriately defined jobs with supervision, training, and rewards, under thoughtful management policies? Volunteers are valuable for illustrating institutional appeal and community support: their presence shows a connection to the community; their work for you demonstrates their support of your mission and priorities. Capitalize on this. Your volunteer cadre is an excellent source for testimonials and community feedback, new ideas, networking, and fundraising. Their interactions outside your museum are an important communication tool—they spread the word about the museum, and they share the local buzz with you. The funder knows a strong volunteer program is a good indication of a strong institution.

If there has been significant staff turnover at the institution, or you have had a recent change in this program area, address that directly by explaining it and describing how you are managing the situation. If your funder is from the community, they likely know that there has been staff turnover. If your funder is specific to our profession, then it and its reviewers are likely to know about the turnover. Make sure you address it in your narrative. Please understand that some funders are reluctant to fund an organization in the first year of a new director's appointment unless the organization or program is well known to them. The funder may be concerned that the project in the request this year might be cut in the future based on new directions for the institution, so a grant early in the director's tenure might have only a temporary impact compared to another later on. To attract new funding during the director's honeymoon period, the project must be critical to core activities and have its own track record, demonstrating that it could function even as the new director is busy getting acquainted with the institution and charts new paths.

Are the Staff and Institution Accredited
or Qualified in Appropriate Ways?

Be sure to highlight the third-party credentials your institution or staff have earned. For staff, this is different from qualifications such as education or experience. This is third-party labeling based on standards set and shared by widely accepted groups. For a fundraiser, it may be a Certified Fund Raising Executive (CFRE), a proposal writer with Grant Professional Certification (GPC), an operations manager who is a Leadership in Energy and Environmental Design Accredited Professional (LEED AP), or a curator who has a PhD. These are not required, but if someone has credentials, be sure to share them when describing your personnel.

For an institution, an obvious sign of credibility is accreditation through AAM, the Association of Zoos and Aquariums, or the appropriate national organization. Accreditation is not a prerequisite for funding, but a funder would understand that the characteristics of an accreditable museum and a fundable institution are related. AAM accreditation "provides credible evidence that the museum not only fulfills its purpose and attains the goals that it proclaims in its mission, but does so in accordance with the highest professional standards." I do not recommend accreditation for funding's sake, but I recommend exploring its appropriateness for improving or maximizing your institution's performance. The process will strengthen your funding case by improving institutional performance and providing you with an easily recognized seal of approval. Since that highest level of performance is not available to all institutions, you can use the StEPs program through AASLH and the Museum Assessment Programs through IMLS, both mentioned in chapter 3, to show that you are working through the standards systems to strengthen your organization. Perhaps you have signed on to the Values of History Statement provided by the History Relevance Committee at AASLH.[2] Your goal is to illustrate that you are aware of standards in the field and that you subscribe to them.

Other forms of field recognition may be more appropriate or more achievable. As a historic property, perhaps you can point to the endorsement of state or national registers. The Argo Gold Mine, Mill and Museum, in Idaho Springs, Colorado, is on the State Register of Historic Places;[3] Andalusia Farm, Home of Flannery O'Connor, is listed on the National Register of Historic Places;[4] and Blithewold Mansion, Gardens and Arboretum can say, based on research and reviews for its Rhode Island and National Register listings, that Blithewold "is nationally significant in American history as one of the most fully-developed and intact examples of the Country Place Era in the United States, and for its high artistic value in representing the influence of the Arts and Crafts movement in this country."[5] *That* gets a funder's attention.

If you have recently built or renovated a building, or are about to, then there are many certification programs that indicate efficiency and environmental sustainability that appeal to most funders. These include the United States Green Building Council's (USGBC) LEED program, the Green Building Initiative's Green Globes Certification program, the International Living Future Institute's Living Building Challenge, or Green Building Certification Institute's SITES Certification program for landscapes. For these, you are likely to achieve certification by working with a landscape professional, engineer, or architect to complete the project and the associated paperwork.

Do you have third-party endorsements to demonstrate that others recognize your value? Can you provide samples of supportive articles or news commentary? If the mayor chose to announce the success of the new historic district program from your site, mention that. She could have chosen anywhere, but your site clearly represented the public appeal and quality that she wanted to communicate to the public, and the gesture means she clearly understands what you do as part of the community. If you win an award for favorite visitor destination from Trip

Dumbarton House, Headquarters of the National Society of the Colonial Dames of America
Dumbarton House/National Society of the Colonial Dames of America, Washington, D.C.

Advisor but that information is incidental to your request for materials for collections storage, then mention the award in the organizational description section of the proposal. When the awards pile up, you will have to choose a select few to make your point as a quality institution, so you can highlight those that align most tightly with the proposal. Dumbarton House won Washington, DC's Mayor's Sustainability Award before the staff successfully applied to the National Endowment for the Humanities for their grant projects and to private funders for the matches. That publicity has continued to open doors for the institution.[6]

Other gifts and grants demonstrate quality, too, as will encouraging comments provided by funders (do ask permission to use them first).

- If you have received a particularly important grant, or one from a prestigious funder, include this in the institutional history section of the proposal (even if the funder asks for a separate list of institutional funders) to show that you've received someone else's valuable seal of approval.

- Perhaps you've received a bequest from someone, or a planned gift commitment that includes a lovely endorsement. Ask the author or the author's family for permission to use that quote specifically in applications. (You'll need permission for other uses as well.)
- Maybe you have begun to receive important gifts of sought-after furniture and documents from the descendants of the original owner of your historic house. This donation demonstrates their support of your work and their confidence in the museum's ability to care for these special pieces.

Less formal endorsements are valuable, too.

- If you have thank-you letters from individuals or groups who were pleased with work you did that is related to this application, include a quotation from them to personalize the case for quality.
- The local newspaper's opinion on your building project, or others' unsolicited public comments on your work, are just as valuable to donors interested in the community.

Can You Demonstrate Programmatic Success?

Now that you've demonstrated the foundation for good work, it's time to demonstrate how you are successful in what you do: prove that you have the knowledge, skills, and ability to address the need well, even better than others can. Evaluation is a powerful tool for providing evidence of success. This book is not a primer on evaluation, but this section is a reminder that evaluation is critical for demonstrating performance worth a funder's investment.

Many agencies and funders (such as IMLS, Americans for the Arts, the United Way, the National Park Service, NEH, NEA, and the Kellogg Foundation, for example) provide valuable tools for measuring changes in values, attitudes, feelings, and knowledge. Visit their websites for the most up-to-date methods.

Sometimes the funder provides an outcome measurement format. If that format does not feel appropriate for your work, then speak to the staff about it before you try to shoehorn your work into their measurement methods. They may agree to your own version of outcome measurement, effectiveness identification, evaluation—whatever you wish to call it. If the funder does not provide a format, then provide your own—one that is appropriate to the work you do and measures the changes that are important to you. Perhaps you want to assess awareness of historical reactions to race issues in the United States, or increase participants' knowledge of midwestern states' geography, or measure repeat visits to the museum by first-time visitors or the success of your efforts to build long-term participation habits or increased circulation in your lending library. Then identify the learning goal and the best way to measure it, and make the case for the appropriateness of that evaluation.

Do You Continue to Improve Your Performance?

Remember, though, evaluation is not just done "on" the visitor or "for" outsiders like grant funders. Evaluation is critical for demonstrating that you are committed to doing your job well, not merely getting it done; it is critical for management. Information collected by measuring outcomes and evaluating exhibits and programs is part of the mix of information that helps you keep your institution investing in the right work for the right reasons. Chapter 6 includes a description of logic models and their use in designing and evaluating program success. Internal review and evaluation can provide direction for staff, identify training needs, and support planning, budget development, and resource allocation decisions. You can apply a logic model to a special event, to an institutional transformational process, and even to a strategic planning process.

No evaluation tool will work unless an institution is ready to accept and address the results; it only works in an environment of honest inquiry, reluctance to find fault, and willingness to use the tool regularly, making it a familiar and expected process. That also means that when the evaluation of a project indicates there are improvements to make or additional opportunities to serve your audience, you can go right ahead and use that as evidence of need in the next proposal to the same funder. You will not be asking for too much of the funder; you will be responding to evaluation information and asking your funder partner to continue to invest in your organization.

Frequent evaluation requires self-discipline, but once the systems are in place and your staff begins to understand the real value of this information, the work becomes easier. On the day you choose *not* to make a decision until you see the evaluation material, you will know that you've internalized this important practice.

ARE YOU A SMART INVESTMENT?

Now that you have proven the need, prove yourself. If you want someone to invest money in your institution, can you show how dependable, stable, and sensible you are? The Ford Foundation has identified signs of institutional weakness that signal a risky investment: chronic cash flow issues, a desperate chase for dollars, dubious funding breakthroughs, an inattentive board, and founder blind spots.[7] If any of these weaknesses are part of your organization's daily struggle, manage those first before preparing grant applications. As foundation officer Ken Ristine points out regularly, you must convince your donor that you are the right choice for this necessary work.[8] Assuring the donor of institutional quality, dependability, and a programmatic return on investment means demonstrating a stable, well-managed institution that adheres to field standards and promises measurable results. Foundation officers ask themselves: Does this museum do something we believe in, with appropriate standards, in a manner we can endorse, that makes effective use of resources for significant, needed change? Can you say that your organization is a good investment?

The Prince Charitable Trusts' support of Blithewold Mansion, Gardens and Arboretum in Bristol, Rhode Island, illustrates how an organization exhibiting the critical characteristics of commitment and ability encouraged a funder. In its early years, Save Blithewold, Inc. (the organization managing Blithewold Mansion, Gardens and Arboretum) approached the Prince Charitable Trusts for support. In summarizing the motivating factor behind the trusts' grants, Kristin Pauly, codirector of the Rhode Island grants program, wrote,

> Blithewold has grown stronger with each year—and it is an organization that has covered all the bases well: important historic site, rare beauty; good management, dedicated staff; broad base of earned income and donations; large cadre of volunteers; well-organized fund-raising events; [and] serious horticulture and professionalism.

Pauly identified quality, stability, planning, support, and management as major factors contributing to Blithewold's appeal. Blithewold continues to attract grants, strengthen the institution, and expand programs because it is gaining credibility *and* has a clear view of what great performance looks like for the institution.

We will start with personnel and operational management, and then follow with financial management.

Are Your Management Practices Clear and Sound?

The experience, attitude, and behaviors of the people who run your institution and its programs are critical. The management practices must be clear and sound. The funder will ask for a board list, often with roles and responsibilities and affiliations. With little effort, the reader will see the size of your board, their areas of expertise and community connections, and the capacities in which they serve at your organizations. The funder is looking for diversity reflecting your audiences, breadth of expertise to guide you effectively, and all the management categories you need to run well. This will reassure them that your organization is shielded from single-focus leadership while regularly refreshing expertise, energy, and support. The next step is to demonstrate how it operates, and that starts with the board and your institutional documents.

Are Your Governing Documents
Appropriate and Up to Date?

This is what the funder is likely wondering as it assesses board-level management:

- Does your board have a coherent, usable structure with clearly defined roles and responsibilities?
- Is it clear from its behavior that it functions as a healthy board by recruiting and training its members, involving each one according to his or her strengths in fulfillment of the organization's mission?
- Does your board's make-up reflect the make-up of the community you serve, such as diversity of wealth, background, region, age, and interests?
- Does it reflect the range of skills you need for good advice?
- Is your board a true help in developing your resources—cash, capital assets, and personnel?

If you are a young or very small organization, it will be helpful to the reader to describe somewhere in the institutional description that you understand board term limits in type and length of service. Be sure either to demonstrate a healthy, working board adhering to the profession's standards or to explain how you plan to achieve this and in how brief a time frame.

Are Your Policies and Procedures Complete?

Policies and procedures are just as critical at a small organization as at a large one. They create dependable and appropriate systems for managing income and expenditures, handling collections, managing volunteers and staff, opening and closing buildings daily or seasonally, renting out spaces, and managing collections. If you do not already have these, then create a priority list for developing them and use the examples available through your state, regional, and national associations to help you develop the most important ones first. You may find a funder, such as your community foundation, willing to provide funding to support the time and effort to refine these for your institution. Once you have basic systems in place that account for health, safety, and security, you can confidently apply for grant projects while steadily developing the other documents.

Do you have guidelines for managing gifts, grants, and investments? We reviewed this in chapter 3, but it bears repeating here. It is critical that you have policies for managing how you process gifts and grants, what the institution gives in return for sponsorships or named gifts, and how you plan to manage investments. Simple documentation supports management consistency while providing a guide to incoming staff or volunteers participating in grant work. You can create your own system; what matters most is that you have one and that it is documented and reviewed. Your work does not end when the envelope comes with the check; that's where responsibility begins.

Codes of behavior demonstrate your understanding of your field's standards and ethics and suggest to the funder that you adhere to them. These include written ethical standards for boards, volunteers and volunteer managers, conservators, fundraisers, and probably many others. Preparing and reviewing specific versions for your institution is an educational process that reinforces the expectations in the codes. The key is to identify the appropriate codes of behavior and performance, articulate them, and follow them. For example, in any institution with physical collections, board and staff personal collecting has ethical ramifications that should be covered by codes of ethics but also by the policies that govern how decisions and consequences are handled at the institution. Attending to investments without conflicts of interest is also critical. Another example is that your institution may choose socially or environmentally responsible investing: you may choose not to invest in some businesses because their actions (such as investment in coal or oil) conflict with your environmental commitment, or you may choose not to host or create certain exhibits because of their tone or because some of the objects are inappropriate. Documenting those choices will simplify the process and establish the policies as the priorities they are rather than vague ideas. You do not need to include copies of your policies and procedures with a proposal, but you can mention in your institutional history that you have a code or codes of behavior for your organization as appropriate for the proposed project, or mention them when those materials provide a case for the proposal under consideration.

Do You Have Appropriate Operating or Strategic Plans?

Can you provide evidence of planning? Planning documents demonstrate reliability and intention. Is there a rationale for your choice of planning tools and how you use them? Like policies and procedures, you will not include these with your proposal, but you must be able to provide them if requested, and refer to them when they support your case. The plans you might use for case making are interpretation, collections, preservation, conservation, investment, strategic, environmental sustainability, succession, disaster, and master plan. If asked, be able to explain how these plans were developed, and how you use them to set goals and monitor progress. If you do not yet have these plans, your regional museum association can probably provide examples and point you to others who have successfully developed plans and may be willing to advise you on their development or recommend good consultants to help you. Please do not copy someone else's plan for the sake of a proposal deadline—the reader will figure it out for sure.

How about Financial Management?

Is your money management and fund development approach appropriate for the institution and the current financial environment? Can you demonstrate fiscal responsibility, transparency, and vigilance? Do you use your resources effectively? What is the rationale for your investment policies, fundraising plan, and budget management? If you have had financial concerns in the past but have addressed them, or are experiencing planned deficits, take the time to explain this to the funder in the proposal. Doing so anticipates a question that, if left unanswered, will derail a grant award, and it avoids unhappy surprises after a grant award if the information comes to light from some other source. Foundation staff can use a museum's financial data as a tool for examining an institution's ability to carry out the proposed work. The funder is interested in an organization's financial history, ability to successfully project financial results, and use of its own data and experience to develop budgets and program plans. These are signs of a thoughtful decision process and planning that promote financial health.

Be prepared to furnish formal documents and an overview of financial management procedures if asked in a proposal. Most museums have either audits or financial compilations prepared by an outside audit firm. The statement of position (SOP), also called a balance sheet, provides key information for determining the assets available to the organization. The SOP classifies assets as unrestricted, permanently restricted, or temporarily restricted. The most important indicators are unrestricted and permanently restricted funds and the level of liabilities or debt. Unrestricted net assets are those that the board may use in whatever way it determines is best for the organization. To determine the amount of unrestricted assets, which the organization can apply toward paying its bills, a funder can deduct the value of property, buildings, and equipment. A negative amount may mean that the museum is experiencing financial difficulties. If the value is less than 20 percent of the organization's operating budget, the organization may have cash flow problems. Permanently restricted assets are donor-specified endowments, and some museums include the value of their collection. Key questions are: Does the organization have an endowment? What is its value, and how has the value changed over time? How much of the endowment does the museum use annually to support operations? What is the ratio of liabilities to assets? How much debt does the organization have? Is the debt short term (to be paid off in less than a year) or long term? How does the amount of the debt relate to the annual operating budget and the organization's net assets?

These are complex questions you will not encounter in an application, but may during a site visit with the funder or in a required financial report related to a grant award. No matter what, understanding your financial situation is critical to both you and the funder in this partnership.

Do You Review Your Financial Condition Regularly?

How well do you manage funds on an annual basis? Audit requirements vary from state to state, and not all states have laws requiring them, but you should know whether you are required to have a review or an audit.[9] If you have an annual audit or compilation, it includes a Statement of Activity (SOA) that indicates the operating revenue and expenses for the fiscal year, and often the previous year as well. A funder can use the data in the SOA to explore questions about the museum's financial management, such as the following: Does the museum have a recent history of operating surpluses or deficits? What is the ratio of earned revenue to contributed revenue? How much of expenses support programmatic efforts? How reliant is the museum on any one funding source or funder? In general, nonprofit organizations are more sustainable if they have a history of annual surpluses and if they are supported by a diverse mix of revenue sources.

Financial data are a key component of the financial assessment funders make as they determine the needs and ability of each organization. Financial information does not stand alone but is considered along with mission, value to the community, response to community needs, and relevance as funders make decisions about how to allocate their finite resources.[10] The answers are in the financial materials that you submit alongside your proposal. The funder will spend as much time reviewing your institution's math as they will the proposal writer's English.

ARE YOU A GOOD PARTNER?

Earlier on we spent time identifying a good mission match between you and the funder in order to attract support. The foundation needs to feel comfortable with the institution as a partner in both appearance and practice, internally and externally. From a partnership point of view, the funder is looking for a behavioral match that promises agreement on values and performance. Matching values and expectations is the basis for a strong and lasting relationship with the donor. A good partner, from the foundation's point of view, is credible, applies its mission internally and externally, provides good public associations and positioning, and will strengthen the donor's reputation.

Mission Priority

From the foundation's point of view, a good partner puts a shared mission into action, says "thank you," manages the program honestly and in communication with the funder, reports truthfully and promptly, and values the relationship beyond the check. The funder can reasonably expect that the mission that drives the work you do in public is reflected in the work you do behind the scenes, and in addition to formal exhibits, programming, and events. Here are examples to consider:

- If you are a preservation organization, show how the organization, you, your staff, or volunteers support the cause in and out of work. Do you attend to the preservation of your own structures? Do you encourage staff to participate on the historical commission or planning board? Does the staff maintain a scenic streetscape or landscape?
- If you are a science museum, are you aware of the science discussions taking place in your community, and do you use them in your exhibit and program research and planning? Do you apply the scientific skills of observation and evaluation in your work?
- If you are a nature museum, do you demonstrate respect for nature in your choice of products and processes associated with running your institution, and do you protect and preserve the natural landscape at your site and in the area?

Did You Manage the Project Well?

We all expect to manage our projects well, and this includes addressing any challenges. If you encounter significant difficulties during the project, ones that limit your reach, make it impossible to deliver a program, or require a significant shift in design, tell your funder. Please do not assume that a funder will abandon you if all does not proceed according to plan. The funder's staff may simply need you to record this as part of the project summary, or they may work with you to make some changes. The staff's considerable experience may be the perspective you need to help you solve your problem. In cases of real trouble, they may become more involved with the project to ensure its success. How you handle adversity is just as important as how you handle projects that proceed according to plan. Remember that your donor is interested in learning as well, and this situation may be an excellent opportunity to do so.

Did You Say "Thank You," and More Than Once?

Yes, funders are busy, so it is important not to waste their time, but most do want a relationship with you, and all appreciate hearing "thank you," so why not use that as an opportunity to build the relationship? When you receive an award, write a thank-you note. You can also call or send an email with thanks, and ask your board members to do the same. Send at least two messages of thanks, preferably three, with at least two from different individuals at your organization. Of course, public announcements of a grant are forms of acknowledgment, but they are not thanks, so they do not count in the recommended two or three you should convey upon hearing of your award. If the grant is a governmental one, and there are city councilors or state or federal legislators to be thanked, they, too, should receive at least two forms of thanks. There is no reason to hold back.

Do You Nurture the Relationship?

Please stay in touch with funders after and in between grants. They may reach out for ideas or ask you to advise another recipient. This is an important way to give back in between requests for funding. To support this new partnership, now and hopefully long into the future:

- provide useful, but not burdensome, updates and meet all funder inquiries happily;
- if some of the students' work is particularly appealing, get permission to send the donor a copy to use in the annual report, to display in their offices, or just to say "thank you";
- if a publication or project they funded wins an award, be sure the donor knows and receives a copy of the award letter; and
- invite them to your site. Even if the funder cannot attend an event or observe the program, they will appreciate the chance to attend if available. It gives them good insight into your work.

ARE YOU A GOOD PARTNER FROM THE OUTSIDE LOOKING IN?

Some might call this the political part of grantmaking. What it means is are you the kind of organization that a funder wants to be associated with? Do you build their credibility through association with you?

Do You Consider the External Situation When Making Decisions?

For so long, museums have been very inwardly focused, but now they are more community focused and are very likely to consider external situations when choosing an exhibit, commenting on the role of monuments in community history and dialogue, selecting board members, and choosing partners. As appropriate, describe this process of considering the social and cultural conditions for your organization (and thereby your donors) when making decisions.

Can You Show How You Contribute to the Community?

Do you, according to your ability, encourage collaboration, and do you participate in community-wide events? Do you give back by encouraging staff to participate on community boards and volunteer in the community? If you charge admission, do you have free days or events? Do you behave in ways that the funder values too?

Can You Demonstrate Successful, Credible Partnerships?

If you attracted early support by partnering with another institution, then you likely already have an example of this. You may have non-grant partnerships to point to, such as long-time school program partners or repeat sponsors for your annual events. And perhaps now others seek you as a partner or provider. These are all examples of how others value you in a partnership, and the funder can as well.

WHAT IS YOUR EDGE?

Lastly, if you want to successfully compete for limited grant dollars, then you need an edge or two. Foundations do not have to fund anything less than the best or what they believe will be the best. Those applicants promising the likeliest, best impact will get the grants. You can do this by multiplying the impact of the investment and by demonstrating that there is a distinct charitable, professional, or innovative edge that distinguishes you from others.

Maximizing the Investment

With so many organizations asking for support, the funder must choose the projects and the organizations likely to make the greatest, most important impact with the funds available. To maximize the impact of the grant, money must achieve multiple goals, and it must "do more than one thing."[11] The applicant that can extend the life or reach of the grant in some way, that maximizes the investment, is more desirable. So when the foundations, corporations, and government agencies ask recipients to explain how their discoveries will be disseminated or the project will be replicated, they are asking how the recipient will maximize impact. Since it is less expensive to reuse a program than to develop it, you can extend impact by offering the program again, minus the planning costs, or help another institution offer it by delivering it too. So, how can you extend the value of your program by repeating, extending, or replicating the project, or helping others to do so? In your case, doing "more than one thing" may mean that:

- An outside lecturer will make a special training presentation to the staff on a specific topic during the afternoon before making the evening presentation to your members and the public on a broader one.
- The project to rehouse the collection will also train an intern in archival care and get the last part of your collection cataloged.
- Support for boiler system replacement will save you money on energy and short-term repairs that can be diverted to the building maintenance fund.
- An energy audit will tell you which efficiency measures will bring you the greatest impact and the fastest return on investment (ROI).
- If you replace all your halogen lightbulbs with the newest version of light-emitting diodes (LEDs), you will save so much money on energy use that you can cut your energy budget by 25 percent, cutting your carbon footprint and saving money to be used on collections and programming.

Another way to improve the funder's return on investment is to extend the grant to others, not financially, but by inviting them to benefit from it as well. This goes beyond creating high internal return on investment in a grant by replicating a program, to increasing the foundation's return on investment by designing ways for others to benefit from the grant to your institution. Here are some examples:

- When the conservation center promises to offer its newly funded textile-cleaning lab to local historical agencies with once-a-month access and supervision, the charitable edge is obvious—the grant award serves multiple audiences.
- If the local government agency helps you bring arts groups to your area, are some of the tickets priced well (or free) so that underserved audiences can attend? Set aside a number of seats for residents at the women's shelter or wards of the juvenile program at city court.
- Invite Social Services to identify two children to benefit from history camperships this summer.
- Share those grant-funded exhibit cases you had installed for your exhibits at town hall with other nonprofits between your installations.
- Invite other nonprofits to use your newly finished second-floor meeting room at given times during the month.
- Allow other collecting institutions to use your new lab once monthly for the cost of materials only.
- When the annual barbecue event has outgrown the front field, share the event and its proceeds with the community parks program if you can fulfill the same goals for your institution and support the parks' goals simultaneously. You can provide management and name recognition while the parks program supplies the larger site and the staff to help with the work.

Reject any argument that you as the recipient institution are giving away something. You are sharing your talents and resources, which enables you and others to do their jobs well while extending the donor's impact. Of course, the charitable action must serve the donor's mission as well as yours and others', and do so without creating a management nightmare or hindering your ability to deliver promises made in the proposal. If the benefit to other organizations outweighs the time it takes you to arrange and supervise the charitable efforts, you will create or strengthen alliances within your community and improve services for more than just your little world. Think of the difference you make by just doing your job.

Does Another Edge Distinguish You?

Beyond ROI, what else distinguishes you among the other strong applicants? There are two nonfinancial "edges" that can interest funders: professional and innovative. It is important to understand how the funder values demonstrated excellence versus innovation.[12] If the funder is a risk taker, it may prefer to see experimental and innovative work. If the funder has a reputation for championing confirmed quality, your proposal should offer a program with a substantial history and powerful endorsements. Most likely you can determine this by reviewing giving guidelines and the descriptions of funded projects. If you are unsure, ask the foundation staff.

Do You Have a Professional Edge?

A professional edge comes from skills and knowledge, either in people or in practice. This is optimum performance. Yes, it's a difficult thing to achieve, but many organizations do it. Your professional edge is a program, process, or product that serves needs in the best way possible while advancing the field.

- Your staff, like Jerry Foust at Dumbarton House, has developed a safe way to reuse plastic political signs for dividers in collections storage. You can share this money-saving practice with others during an exhibits and collections-care-on-a-shoestring workshop.
- Because of a recent hurricane-related flood, you are now prepared to share your successful preparation and recovery practices with other agencies in the region that did not fare as well.
- You have made interpretation of a people your focus with such distinction that you can attest—as the Whitney Plantation in Wallace, Louisiana, can attest to its slavery story—that your

work has rigorousness and authenticity that no other site in the region can offer.

- Your archival collection has natural history records that are being included in climate change assessment work by the local university, giving you an opportunity to create an exhibit through science and history that illustrates a global discussion on a local scale. No other museum in the area has this data.

Do You Have an Innovative Edge?

This is where you add new knowledge to the field. Your innovation may be finding new partners and new ways to use oral history in collecting and exhibiting information, involving volunteers and new partners, or collaborating locally, regionally, or nationally. Why is innovation important? Let's say that your proposal makes the first cut in the selection process, and the second, but when the review committee sits around the table for final decisions and many components are equal among the surviving proposals, innovative proposals will be the most appealing. Yes, it is hard to keep up with our work and have time to innovate, but many are doing it. Your innovation may be in attitude, style, or method. Remember when the trend began for curators to emphasize education, not just connoisseurship? How about when gift shops were encouraged to align their wares with the museum's collections and educational mission? These were once novel ideas. Now the novel approaches are dialogic programs, and advocacy instead of neutrality. Innovation may be how you differentiate yourself from other museums or attractions. "Innovative" is defined by your circumstances and your goals. They may be changes in institutional behavior, a stretch to a new level of collections care, or new practices or programs on a local or regional level. Innovation does not need to be on a national or global scale.

- Have you incorporated audio, visual, or physical features into your exhibits in a way that is unusual for museums, or that explores the use of cutting-edge technology or social media, or is it a new immersion approach?
- Do you have a new approach to interpreting your historic house based on new research or new partnerships?

- Have you chosen an unusual, newly interpreted, or overlooked focus for some of your work?
- Are you testing a new cooperative admission ticket for your community?

To strengthen your case, you will need to provide some perspective. This helps your donor understand your reasoning for your innovation, and also the scale and impact. Your goal is to demonstrate how you have conscientiously addressed challenges with appropriate new thinking. For many, an outward-thinking, confident organization is an asset as a partner.

Professional edge and innovative edge will often overlap. For example, the research by the Image Permanence Institute for Rochester Institute of Technology in Rochester, New York, has a professional edge over anyone else in the field for understanding the effects of temperature and relative humidity on the mechanical, chemical, and biological degradation of artifacts. The information they provide benefits collecting institutions and those with historic structures. Developing that information was their innovative edge; sharing it is their professional edge. It is the same in the case of the Abbe Museum. Its edge is the quality of its collaboration with Wabanaki people. It is transforming the entire definition of its interaction with the five tribes—Penobscot, Passamaquoddy, Micmac, Maliseet, and Abenaki—who have communities in New England and Eastern Canada. It is fostering that transformation through decolonization.

This quote from the museum's strategic plan is an ideal case statement for the museum's professional edge. Its strength now attracts invitations for grant applications from foundations that otherwise only accept applications from preselected organizations.

Decolonization is the Abbe Museum's touchstone and guiding principle: it is committed to an ongoing process of better understanding Wabanaki culture, history, and values and examining and changing its practices to assure they reflect those values. This is an emerging concept in museum practice in the United States and the Abbe Museum is deeply committed to work that positively impacts the tribal communities and the museum industry. The Abbe is already a resource and a model that the museum

The Abbe Museum, Bar Harbor, Maine

field turns to for ideas, solutions, and strategies for comprehensive museum decolonization and the board and staff will deepen and broaden that commitment.[13]

That is innovative, and though the staff would look at it as a responsibility rather than an edge, by sharing that responsibility with the field and training others in the fulfillment of it, it is the museum's professional edge. What is important is the existence of an edge, not the labeling of it.

CONCLUSION

Perhaps because we know in our own hearts that we are doing our very best, and that a little help can make all the difference, we grow impatient with explaining the situation yet again in each proposal. That is understandable, but irrelevant. What you cannot afford through earned income you must earn through grants. When you apply for a grant, you are asking the funder to make an investment in your organization. Such a commitment requires due diligence on both sides of the check. You

earn grant income by developing and cultivating productive relationships with funders by understanding their needs, interests, and expectations; providing excellent and/or innovative programming to address
shared missions; managing funded projects well; and preparing useful
and readable proposals. By demonstrating your worthiness for this
investment, you simplify the due diligence process for the foundation
and demonstrate your knowledge of proper responsibilities and behavior associated with the trust they are being asked to bestow. There is
no substitute. It all comes down to "Will they want to work with you
again?" Make sure the answer will always be "yes."

NOTES

1. Sarah Lyall, "Off the Beat and Into a Museum: Art Helps Police
Officers Learn to Look," *New York Times*, April 26, 2016, https://www
.nytimes.com/2016/04/27/arts/design/art-helps-police-officers-learn-to-look
.html?_r=0.

2. "Value of History," History Relevance, accessed October 19, 2017,
https://www.historyrelevance.com/value-history-statement/.

3. Colorado Historical Society, Office of Archaeology and Historic Preservation, *Museum Buildings, Sites and Structures on the Colorado State Register of Historic Properties*, 2008, 12, http://www.historycolorado.org/sites
/default/files/files/OAHP/crforms_edumat/pdfs/1639.pdf.

4. "About Us," Andalusia Farm, accessed April 7, 2017, http://andalusiafarm
.org/about-us/.

5. "About the Estate," Blithewold, accessed April 7, 2017, http://www
.blithewold.org/about/the-estate/.

6. "Dumbarton House Receives 2013 Mayor's Sustainability Award,"
Dumbarton House, accessed October 19, 2017, http://dumbartonhouse.org
/2013-mayors-sustainability-award.

7. GrantCraft, *When Projects Flounder* (New York: Ford Foundation,
2003), 3–4.

8. Ken Ristine of the Ben B. Cheney Foundation gets full credit for articulating this important step in the process.

9. "State Law Nonprofit Audit Requirements: Does Your State's Law Require an Independent Audit?" National Council of Nonprofits, accessed April
7, 2017, https://www.councilofnonprofits.org/nonprofit-audit-guide/state-law
-audit-requirements.

10. The entire section on assessing financial stability was provided by Sally Zinno, management and financial consultant to arts and cultural organizations.

11. Hope Alswang, the New York State Council for the Arts and Advisory Council Member, Concord Museum, Massachusetts, during the late 1980s.

12. Thank you to management consultant Laura Roberts for her comments on the importance of recognizing the values of excellence and innovation as often separate goals.

13. Grant application to the Institute of Museum and Library Services, 2016.

CHAPTER 5

Logic Models and Budgets
Are Your Friends

Now that your organization is ready for grants, let's be sure your design process is tuned to design fundable projects. That is where logic models and budgets come in: they are a proposal writer's best friends. They provide a reliable format for organizing information and, most important, direct the focus of your work with your colleagues. In the same way that an agenda keeps a meeting on task and moving along, the blanks in the logic model and budget keep the proposal team asking and answering important questions as you refine the project. This is an important process for a letter of inquiry, concept paper, or proposal, and for implementation if funded, so don't put these off thinking you only need them if you're submitting a full proposal. Do them first, and you'll be grateful throughout the whole process.

USING A LOGIC MODEL

Let's start with the logic models, since they're practically a two-for-one activity. Completing one requires you to list and organize the actions, resources, and results for your project and then transfer them into your proposal. This process gives you a list of components—many you will describe in the proposal, and most will be part of your budget. Very few funders require you to submit a logic model, but completing one saves time because it simplifies the writing process by organizing much of your content in outline form. The bonus is that completing the logic model first will make the budget process far easier, too. As you list what you need and whom you serve, how much of both are part of the project, and what you're doing and what you need to do it, you're creating the structure for your budget and making sure nothing gets overlooked.

There is no one way to organize a logic model, but they all have the same basic components and occasional additions. First, let's understand the components; then we can fill in blanks. The usual components are:

Inputs: the things you need to do this project.
Activities: the things you do during the project and to make this project happen.
Outputs: the people you will reach and the things you want to produce during this project.
Outcomes: the changes you expect because of this project.

For many writers, the inputs and activities are simple enough, but distinguishing between outputs and outcomes is harder. Here's a simple way to manage it: remember that outputs are people and products; outcomes are changes in conditions, capacity, values, attitudes, and feelings that are the results of your work. Example: Earl Kawa'a teaches Native Hawaiian families how to fashion poi boards and pounders for making the traditional Hawaiian food staple from taro. The classes teach tradition, history, and a "family-first" attitude that Kawa'a sees has eroded and is eroding in Hawaiian life today. When he talks about what comes out of the experience, he says, "The Keiki O Ka'Aina [child of the land/Native Hawaiian] classes are designed to make the board and stone, so that's the physical result, but it's also about shaping attitudes and behavior for family unity and lifelong-learning. What happens is there's a change in attitude and behavior." In Earl Kawa'a's project, the board and stones are products, the outputs; the new attitude and behavior is the change, the outcome.[1]

In a logic model there are often categories for segmenting outputs and outcomes into near term, midterm, and long term. This is usually more important in documenting change (outcome) because although change may take time beyond the grant period, it can still be part of the case for the project. Kawa'a's goal is for his "'graduates' to continue their journey toward increased cultural awareness and family bonding," all of which takes more than this workshop to make a poi board and pounder, but it has a solid foundation there. Kawa'a offers additional

Table 5.1. Sample Logic Model for a Program: Example Is Poi Boards and Poi Pounders

Use inputs, activities, and participation to help plan your budget.

The bold text identifies the desired changes (outcomes) created through the program based on its focus for strengthening families.

	Outputs (Products)		Outcomes (Impact/Changes)		
Inputs	Activities	Participation	Short	Medium	Long
Program leader's time for collecting materials and leading family workshops	Focused family time	# of families participating in workshops	**Learning as a family** to make poi boards and pounders	Families report plans to use board and pounders for making **poi for special family occasions**	Family continues to pursue discovery of traditional practices
Office staff for scheduling, sign-ups	Learning about historical practices that have relevance today	# of families reporting plans to use board and pounders for making poi	**Family discussions** of traditional practices and foodways and how to incorporate them into modern life	Participants report **increased understanding** of, and respect for, traditional Hawaiian practices	**Family continues to pursue activities together**
Materials for pounders and boards	Family discussions of the role and value of family in traditional and modern life	# of families returning for future workshops	**# of families reporting increased interest** in traditional family practices	**# of families reporting interest** in attending future workshops	
Historical examples and images of pounders and boards for explanation		# of geographic areas served			
Workshop spaces around the state (no chairs or tables needed, but shade covering is important)		# of different agencies requesting workshops			
Promotional information and materials for print and online promotion					

programs for his "graduates" that build on this first one. That design reinforces the funders' confidence that the desired change can be accomplished even though the grant may not last that long.

In addition to the inputs, activities, outputs, and outcomes, some logic models include sections for noting underlying conditions or assumptions that influenced the design or may affect the results. You could describe these as the hypothesis, or the case. The assumptions and conditions help explain the "why" of the project. In Kawa'a's example, the underlying condition is that, within his seventy-year-old memory, 90 percent of families pounded poi at home, but he could only locate a few known stones and boards on the island when he wanted to start his program. His assumptions are that learning the history of poi and poi pounding, the process of creating the stones and boards (and eventually poi), and doing so together can create a valuable family bonding experience that is an important building block for strengthening family connection through values. For your project, thinking through the assumptions and underlying conditions can help you articulate the "why" for your project. Putting them in the logic model keeps the "why" connected to the "how" once it's time to write your proposal and then implement the program.

A PRACTICE LOGIC MODEL

Some writers rank logic models with budgets at the top of the list of anxiety-making processes. To fix that, let's practice a user-friendly approach by choosing a nonmuseum focus, something much simpler and more familiar than a new grant project: a family reunion to celebrate a milestone birthday. After doing this just once with the sample event, it should make it easy to substitute museum-oriented components in the model when you use it in the future. So now, without overthinking it, imagine sitting around the table with some of your family, beginning to plan your father's eightieth birthday and a simultaneous family reunion. What do you need to make this party happen?

A place, with enough room for everyone and the activities.

Is it at your home? At his place? At a rented venue? At a destination? Do people come for a short or long time? Do they stay overnight? How do they get there? How much of that are you responsible for?

It's at a sister's home because she has space, which saves money, but only Mom and Dad can stay there; everyone else is on their own to travel and make overnight arrangements. The gathering lasts from afternoon until late evening.

So, no travel arrangements are part of this project, or rental spaces. What equipment do you need?

We can cook lots of the food at her house, but not all of it; people will have to bring food or we can order some. And we'll need some extra chairs and tables, some of those pop-up tents, and coolers for drinks.

This is good thinking. Those items you need are all *inputs*; getting and setting them up, not to mention acquiring the food supplies and cooking, are all activities—so now it's time to start noting a few things under *activities*. When beginning to consider expenses, you can use this list to estimate what you need to buy, how much of it, and how much it all costs. If you were planning an event in a grant proposal, you would use that estimation for budgeting, and you'd use the activities to calculate time needed and therefore the cost of paying for the staff, service provider, or consultant time.

We need stuff for the party: invitations, decorations, food and drinks, a cake and ice cream, yard games plus inside games for the little ones once it gets dark. There is going to be a lot of garbage; we need containers for garbage and recycling.

Right, and who's going to do all this? Under *activities* you now have decorating, organizing games, handling the trash and recycling, and watching the kids. When you assign those jobs, you will be identifying family members who would be the "personnel" in a grant proposal and would need places in the budget.

Let's move on to *outputs*, because those will feedback into inputs and activities. How many people and which people will this reach? And what will the party produce? Beyond the obvious food and drink, which we will just call refreshments, is there something more important? Are you going to create a family album—a virtual one for all the family, and a hard copy for Dad? Are you going to use the event to swap baby clothes and teach the youngest ones to play football? If yes, then your outputs/products are family albums, a clothes-swap event, and a family football game.

The clothes-swap and the football game feel like activities rather than things.

Good point. If the actions are required to create the party—which is the main output/product—then they're an *activity*; if they happen as part of the party, they're an *output*/product of the party—they just happen to be kinetic, not static, products.

This discussion has led you to think about changes, the *outcomes*. During the party you will create and revive memories—products that will cultivate feelings of celebration, remembrance, and connection. These are outcomes that have value; they are *the* change you want to result from your event. Because you are creating the album to share, you will be extending the value of your reunion to those who couldn't come and into time after the event. Be sure to include all those you reach in your outcomes.

Because of the clothes swap, the outcome will also be that family members have clothing they need, with less cost. It is likely that during the swap they will create stories and remembrances that reinforce the goals of the party. The same will happen during the football game as parents and uncles and aunts remember and share stories and practices.

With all this remembering and connecting going on, it sounds as if one of the goals of this activity serves family members, not just Dad. You're all there to celebrate Dad's birthday, but you're also creating a family experience where members share knowledge and memories—which means each one is likely to build more of their own.

Often during this process, you will begin to feel that there are more outputs and outcomes than you can or want to track. Before distilling them, segment all the outcomes and outputs into time frames. A short-term outcome is that everyone is together for the first time in nine years. Some mid-term ones are that three families now have an infusion of clothing they don't have to shop for, and the real and virtual albums revive connections among you all. A long-term one is that you have a lasting family record that, if done to support this goal, will include information about who is who, how they're related, and a little of their story.

If at some point you find that there are more outputs and outcomes than you can or want to track, that's when, in the grant proposal, you would focus on those that you confirm are the top priorities for the project and the funder.

A MUSEUM EXAMPLE

Let's try the same exercise on a museum program. This is a new school program for grade 6 on United States history. You'll be taking the approach that learning how to research local history and place it in the national history pageant addresses multiple goals, including satisfaction of state curriculum requirements for national history and mission-focused goals of promoting the use of local resources to develop twenty-first-century skills. Your education program focus is that learning to interpret history builds skills for assessing the accuracy and relevance of information, and for using information appropriately.[2] The process teaches students how to recognize multiple perspectives and biases, analysis of conflicting evidence, and the importance of sequencing to identify causes—all skills identified as critical to a successful and productive life in the twenty-first century.[3]

Inputs

The inputs would be museum staff, space, students, teachers, all the primary and secondary materials for research, and likely some exhibit space for exhibiting students' work and making end-of-program presentations to classmates and family. You might be more specific and state the exact collections you'll be providing. These inputs may make your program particularly distinctive, so highlight them. If you're choosing to provide access to a new collection of town records relating to land use and planning in the nineteenth and twentieth centuries, you may need to make copies or enlargements and laminate them for students' use. Maybe you've decided that in addition to the educators leading the program, you'll invite a local resident who can talk about how she uses historical research in her work as a planner for the town, something that brings the research into the twenty-first century. This person is an input in your logical model.

If you're offering a program for the third time around, and this year you're adding a segment that includes a neighboring town that has recently been added to the school district, make sure the work to prepare the addition is included in this year's logic model, as it will affect time and effort in the project design. Each time you write about a project, check or rewrite the logic model to make sure it reflects the project.

Activities and Inputs

This program is about research, but let's break down "research" into all its component activities. The students will need an orientation on how to conduct the research process and use original documents and secondary materials, time to conduct research on their own, and time to develop their conclusions and create their end products. These activities require staff and teacher supervision, transportation to the site, and access to the collections, plus time, space, and materials for their final projects. Those activities tell you to plan bus transportation as an input and enough time and money for staff to plan for collections access, deliver training, and provide support. Preparing the facsimiles requires staff time and money.

Research is the core activity, but there are related ones to include. The local resident's presentation will require planning and a place for the presentation. The exhibits and students' presentation will require space, so both of those must go under inputs. Preparing the exhibits will require materials that should go under inputs and have a cost in the budget.

Outputs and Outcomes

Since this is the first time you've used this collection in a program, one product is the new facsimiles; one outcome is that they will now be available for continued use in subsequent programs, with less cost to those programs. But how are you going to measure changes in values, attitudes, feelings, and understanding? On a programmatic level, you may set the outcomes as they relate to:

- increased awareness of the types of records available for historical research, and how historical records inform modern practice
- improved ability to discern unbiased information, the "voice" of the person creating the document based on practice at the time, and the expectations of someone interpreting it from second-hand information
- improved ability to recognize differing approaches and uncover the conditions creating those approaches or viewpoints using the documents
- improved ability to sort and sequence information to develop a more complete picture of the event or topic, and conditions surrounding it

You can measure improvement through pretesting and post-testing, asking students to rate their awareness and assess their abilities. To create measurable objectives and evaluate effectiveness, you'll establish criteria for the students' learning and projects and create estimates for the percentage of students able to fulfill that criteria. You can set short-term goals for this project, but if this is part of a sequence of activities with the school, you may have other programs that build on each other and may set mid-term and long-term goals monitoring students' progress.

To document outputs such as students reached and work completed, you can design the project to reflect the content and structure of specific portions of the state's learning curriculum for that age group, then measure the number of students who participate and complete the work. You can also photograph or capture digital versions of the students' work as products.

For assumptions and conditions, that category at the bottom of the page and running across the width of your columns, you may choose to make the case that modern access to maps and images means students have no practice reading maps or finding routes in the context of the landscape or interpreting what the mapmaker chooses to record and why. This makes it critical for students to learn and relearn the skills of assessing information for drawing responsible conclusions and making thoughtful decisions, and that guided practice is an important way to establish these skills.

If you'd like another chance to practice a logic model on your own, try filling out one for a program you know well and have been running for a long time at your organization. This will make filling in the blanks quite easy. Then, when you use the process on a new project and proposal, it will be a breeze to complete.

THE BUDGET

This, of course, is something you *will* submit to the funder, even for most letters of inquity (LOIs). It's another way the funder can see the detail and scope of your work and gauge its potential for success based on the sufficiency of components and funding of those components. Almost all funders provide a budget form for you to download, complete, and return with the proposal. Many use a common format developed with their regional funders network. They will give you a link to this if they require it. If they do not give you a budget format and you do not wish to create your own, you can use the regional funders' format, downloading it for free from the network website.

Often the common format includes dual budget sections on a one-page form so that the funder can see the project budget and the institutional budget at the same time. Government agencies often ask only for the project budget and the totals for institutional expenses and income for a fiscal year. Those agencies also provide a budget form to guide you, and instructions that include definitions of words that may be unfamiliar. If you still have questions—for government agency or private funder application—call the funder. They'd rather deal with budget issues before the money is allocated or spent.

The most important part of the budget is the calculating you do to get your numbers. So, show your math wherever possible, and keep a copy of those notes for yourself, the project director, and your financial person. Making one for each proposal is a great idea—government agency or not. When the grant comes in, you all will have forgotten these details and need some frame of reference for allocating funds. Government agencies usually ask for a budget narrative that includes these calculations. You don't need to make notes to yourself about the institutional budget; presumably that information is recorded somewhere else. The categories you're likely to see in a budget are:

- staff (or salaries and wages, often with fringe benefits broken out)
- consultants
- materials and supplies
- equipment
- space rental
- marketing and advertising
- permits and fees
- printing/copying/postage
- miscellaneous

To complete your budget form, work through each section calculating all the individual components; then add them up into the single line item space provided. Do this with the logic model in front of you so that you remember to include all the components and so that you can use your earlier notes and calculations to help fill in the blanks. So, if your logic model for a series of grade 6 research programs, for all four schools in the county during the fall and spring semesters, names three staff members—one at 10 percent time on a salary of $70,000, one at 25 percent time on a salary of $35,000, and one for three hundred hours at $12 per hour, all over a period of six months—then your total line item for staff is $7,000 + $8,750 + $3,600, or $19,350.

Fill out what you can. Usually there is space for self-defined categories if you have significant expenses for a category and you would like to isolate the amount. For example, if your programs include consumables, you might separate out the amount for food for your hearth cooking sessions, but you would not isolate the incidentals such as paper towels, soap, hand sanitizer, and utensils. Generally, it's worth identifying items or groupings that are 5 percent of your budget or valued at $5,000 or above.

Remember that a budget is not just expenses but income as well—and they should equal each other. The categories you may see are:

- government grants
- foundation/corporate grants

- individual contributions
- earned income
- in-kind support
- other

If the local bus company donates transportation and the local printer donates the copying and laminating, those go under "in-kind" income. If the local bank donates $1,000 and the community foundation donates $5,000, both go together under foundation/corporate grants. If the town donates $1,000, that goes under government grants. When a parent who is also a volunteer hears about the program and donates $500 to the project, that goes under individual contributions. Chapter 3 has more on how to build out this part of the budget even when you are not exactly sure where all the income will come from.

When you're done with your budget, be sure to have someone else review not only your math but also all of the components. This will ensure that it's complete and correct and will likely eliminate any surprises once the proposal is funded.

CONCLUSION

This should give you a strong start on describing your project in your letter of inquiry, concept paper, or proposal. Now we'll determine which it will be.

NOTES

1. Jason Genegabus, "Shaping Hearts & Minds," *Honolulu Star-Advertiser Sunday Magazine,* June 18, 2017, 6.

2. Samuel S. Wineburg, *Historical Thinking and Other Unnatural Acts: Charting the Future of Teaching the Past* (Philadelphia: Temple University Press, 2001); Samuel S. Wineburg, "Historical Thinking Matters," accessed August 25, 2017, https://sheg.stanford.edu/htm.

3. "Value of History," History Relevance, accessed August 25, 2017, https://www.historyrelevance.com/value-history-statement/.

CHAPTER 6

Your Proposal-Writing Process

There are two parts to writing. Up until now we have discussed the product; what about the less predictable process—getting the words on the page according to the proposal needs? The writing process is distinctive to each of us. What matters most is that you are conscious of developing a method of writing as best you can and as efficiently as possible during the grants process.

BUILDING SKILLS

Though some people are drawn to writing, it is a skill anyone can learn if they care to. Improving your work requires practicing your writing in proposal and other formats, as well as a good foundation of wide-ranging personal and professional reading. A good background in the humanities helps, and everyone can benefit from a friendly critique when not under the pressure of a deadline.

If you want to check your punctuation skills and word use, arrange to have a writing teacher, or someone more experienced in professional writing, review a few of your proposals with you. Grammarly.com is a free grammar-checking website, and the perennial *Elements of Style* by William Strunk Jr. and E. B. White, now in its fourth edition, is a valuable resource. Lynne Truss's *Eats, Shoots and Leaves* is one of the funniest writing books ever, and it's very helpful. *Writing for a Good Cause* by Joseph Barbato and Danielle Furlich will help you out of any writing slump, and it is valuable for any writing you do on behalf of your museum. Reading one or two of those books a year, and rereading them, is important professional development.

To focus on grant skills, build experience by reading others' proposals. Government agencies often have good proposals on their websites since those proposals all become a matter of public record, but private grants are harder to access. One of the best ways to learn about the good and bad ways to write and prepare proposals is to be a proposal reviewer for a local arts agency, a community foundation, or a federal program such as IMLS. The reading load will be hefty, but you will learn a great deal and support a thoughtful funding process. You will quickly come to see which writing styles and formats are most helpful to a reader. The whole experience will be very valuable to you and the community of recipients.

A WRITING PLACE

Do you prefer to write in silence, with white noise, or in chaos? Do you sit down or stand up? Do you need a cleared desk, or a different desk, to be comfortable and ready to write? Can you tolerate interruptions? If you take time to assess these preferences, you will quickly find the most helpful arrangement. Of course, only some aspects are under your control, and some preferences apply in differing situations, but still, your brain and process will be more effective if you create a good work setting—whether or not the task at hand is writing.

I choose to listen to music without words when I'm creating new text, and white noise when I'm attending to detail. I write new material or tackle broad concepts best when standing because it's a more creative stance and I can move around a bit. I edit, or write, difficult material best sitting down and paying attention to detail. When I have something to describe that is complex, then I need silence with zero interruptions.

If you have space for more than one desk, having one for writing and one for other work, or one for standing and one for sitting (or adjustable), can be very helpful. Or you may have a favorite coffee shop or porch to head to for writing. You may simply need to hang a "Do not disturb" sign on your door. If you don't have a door, headphones with music can help, as does a sign on the back of your chair saying,

"Shhh, raising money for your salary!" Many proposal writers have an arrangement where they can work from home for writing. If you are disciplined when working offsite or at home, this is a great option. I have found that when I begin to allow all other conceivable activities to interfere with my writing time, then I need to go somewhere with only enough materials and information for working on the project at hand.

If at all possible, write when you are fresh and interested, or focused by a close but reasonable deadline. Your writing will surely be clearer. Whether you block off full mornings, promise yourself an hour first thing each day, work the whole weekend when the office is empty, or work at home when the office is full, make a point of creating the time and space to focus.

GETTING IT DONE

Writing an LOI or Proposal from Scratch

For starting a new proposal, it makes no difference whether you are the kind of writer who crafts every sentence carefully before moving on to the next or you are the kind who throws all the information on the page at first and then goes back over it repeatedly. The time factor may be the same for both anyway. The key is to get yourself ready and writing as effectively as you can, given your style and your resources. With experience, you will refine the process as a balance between style and time. This sequence seems the most efficient:

- skim, then *dissect* the guidelines
- begin collecting all support letters, budget information, and attachments
- connect with staff or colleagues who are preparing support letters, adding to the budget, or creating estimates
- do the discovery work to collect resources and build the knowledge you will use to create the text
- sit with the project team to create the logic model
- build a budget, and align all its components with the proposal
- organize all the information in your document, sequencing the proposal questions and the topics for your planned response

- write and rewrite text sections (see sidebar for examples)
- share with necessary staff and informal reviewers, then rewrite and reshare, then edit
- finish by proofing and submitting

To start your proposal, you need all the materials that support your application. So, begin the process by skimming the guidelines and the application format to be sure you know what you need. This will orient you to the language and style of the funder, and help you establish expectations for the components and complexity of the proposal. I copy them into the proposal draft for early reference, and then delete them at the end when I am sure all the components are included. I wait as long as I can to remove these instructions. If a peer reads your material, or you do weeks later, one of you may be tempted to cut a section to save space. If you still have the instructions embedded, you can double check to be sure you are not cutting a critical piece.

Then reread the guidelines very carefully, highlighting everything that is too risky to forget—page length and font, for example—or that you are likely to lose track of as you write, such as evaluation criteria. Create the to-do list of any people to invite for participation or endorsements and get those started early so they don't hold you up at the end. You may need to ask someone for supporting images or materials; you may need an estimate for a budget item or a memorandum of understanding (MOU) from a partner. For a federal grant, you may realize that you have not updated your grants.gov password recently or that the Authorized Organization Representative (AOR who submits the grant after you write it) has changed since you last applied and you need to get them signed up. All of these chores should be accomplished immediately so that you are free to create and are not caught at the end waiting on missing details you could have addressed at the beginning. Please make sure you give yourself enough days to collect information and contact others so that the final product isn't a rush.

That means you must begin the process early. If it's a proposal or LOI to a private foundation for an existing project, you may only need a month's time for all the details and review, whereas a new project takes at least two months' time to design well. A federal proposal needs at least two months, preferably three or four, in lead time simply for the scope and complexity of the project. If you are designing a new project with partners, the process may be six months long.

You are not writing all that time, but developing, collecting, and preparing as you begin your drafts. Usually federal guidelines appear as a Funding Opportunity Announcement (FOA) only six weeks before the proposal is due. You can start preparing early by using the previous year's FOA, likely archived on the website, for the basics, and calling to talk with the program officer about your project and to find out whether they suspect or expect any significant changes to the guidelines. Be sure to submit your email address so that you are updated on any changes.

Then make sure you have all the information you think you need to help you write. This means the reports from similar programs that have already been completed, along with any references that demonstrate research supportive to your approach; a solid understanding of the who, what, where, when, and why of the project; and a clear understanding of the outputs and outcomes and how you will measure and evaluate them. Sometimes this process of "discovery"—collecting all the right information—helps you identify information gaps or unfinished design aspects to the proposal. Usually, the process also primes your writing mind with information, ideas, and language that will help you launch into writing. The more complete the discovery process is, the smoother the writing process will be.

The discussion in the previous chapter demonstrated how you can use the experience of building the logic model and budget to prime you for describing the project in the proposal. The usual recommendations are to outline the proposal before you start, and to have someone who is not associated with the project read it when you are done. The former is efficient; the latter is a great fail-safe for creating intelligible text. Both recommendations are often very hard to accomplish. I offer them as examples of best practice we can all aspire to. Having someone else read your proposal for clarity is especially important when you write about a topic for the very first time, or you write about it for the twentieth time.

The first time you describe a program or project, your language may be imprecise because you are still mentally refining the description. You may use more jargon because that is easier than using simpler, more descriptive language; you may make assumptions about the topic the reader doesn't understand; and you may be so enamored of this new idea or project that you overdo the writing.

The opposite happens when you are writing on the topic for the twentieth time. If it is too familiar, and you are tired and bored of the text, then your mind creates its own shortcuts, leaping ahead to known information and making it seem as if the written word is overdone. When this happens, you are likely to start cutting back and leaving out material that others require to understand the unfamiliar topic. However, if you don't have someone well suited to read for you, then plan to take at least a day or two away from your work. When you return to it, you will likely be more attentive and therefore apt to notice any gaps or awkwardness in the material.

When you are crafting text, if you get stuck in an area, or you really struggle with how to describe a part or all of the project, there are likely two reasons: either you don't understand it well enough yet or you love the way the words sound even though they don't really make the proposal stronger. To solve the first problem, turn back to talking with someone to learn more about the program, getting out to observe it or doing your own research to build your knowledge and understanding. When you return to write about it, the process is likely to be much easier.

Often we develop an attachment to words or a sequence of words that otherwise interrupts and complicates. The best antidote is to cut out the section, paste it in the "parking lot" you create at the end of the document, and then rewrite that part from scratch as if you had to explain it out loud to a classroom of high school students not enrolled in museum studies. That will help you simplify it. You can go back and smooth it into the paragraph after you get the idea restated and the block removed. If it turns out that the text you cut is needed later, it is waiting for you in the parking lot. You can run a quick test to see whether your writing has gone too far in the direction of explanations and jargon. Sherilyn Young, a proposal writer for the United Keetoowah Band of Cherokee, says that your material must "catch their eye, stir their mind, and warm their heart." Does yours? When the John Hair Cultural Center in Tahlequah, Oklahoma, submitted a proposal to the IMLS Native American/Native Hawaiian Services program in 2016, it used that approach. The application for the project, "Missing Pieces: Documenting Keetoowah Heritage," was successful. This is a paragraph from the proposal's first introductory page:

The John Hair Cultural Center and Museum
Photo by Sammy Still

What need, problem, or challenge will your project address and how was it identified?
On a hot, hot July day, Ernestine Berry, Executive Director of the JHCCM, and a MAP I reviewer visited [a nearby museum]. While touring collections storage with the curator, the group discussed the heat and the difficulty keeping the collections area dehumidified, and the backlog of collections processing. On their way out, Berry saw, for the first time in her life, the enrollment cards for the Keetoowah people. They were unceremoniously stored at the end of a row of shelves, overlooked and unprocessed, in the busy front passage of the storeroom. These are missing pieces.

Writing an LOI or Proposal with Existing Content

There is a myth out there that you can store and reuse "boilerplate" material, or long-lasting and universal content, for multiple proposals and that only a few details need be tweaked to "customize" the proposal. This is entirely untrue. Some facts, phrases, and explanation sequences may transfer well, but the story does not. When reusing text from a previous proposal, the hardest part is creating a natural flow within the new set of questions, creating something complete and smooth while cutting and pasting from the old proposal. Elizabeth Wylie, longtime museum curator and director, is experienced in proposal review for grants, awards, and national conferences. She says that the difference between a well-planned, carefully crafted proposal and a just-the-basics response is night and day to the reviewer. The best proposals flow like a story instead of like a call-and-response march through the narrative questions. "I enjoy reading, and think well of, applications that use short sentences, avoid jargon, and state clearly and plainly where the organization has been, where it is, and where it intends to go if funded. I like to see the thought that identified the intended path and why it is important to the organization, to the community, and to the funders. It's revealing when applicants use all available real estate (i.e., word count) to tell the story and not waste it with cut-and-paste repetition."[1]

The call-and-response feel is an unfortunate byproduct of a proposal format with a series of set questions you must complete. Here's what usually happens: to be sure you remember each one, it is likely that you will cut and paste the questions, in bold headers, into the document, keeping the criteria pasted there, too, during the first drafts. Then you will write up the content for each section below the bold header. That makes for very choppy material, but a complete answer. To smooth it out, when you are ready to read through it all for the first time, turn the headers from bold to light gray, and read through without focusing on the questions, but rather on the flow of the answers. How smooth is it? Does something get repeated or should something be moved? Does it flow reasonably well from the end of one section to the beginning of the next? Can you tell the priority intent of each section? After you rewrite it and feel it is smooth, then you can add back the bold headings and recheck that you have covered all of the required content for each question.

Writing an LOI or Proposal to Continue a Project

An application to continue a project is a hybrid of a new project proposal and a new format for an old proposal. In this case, you can use the previously submitted proposal, but with care. First, review all the current guidelines and questions and attachments to identify any difference from the previous submittal. Then work through the old proposal noting where you can refresh participation and budget numbers, add results, and include anecdotes from assessments to enliven your case and demonstrate what you learned and what was most valuable. You might include new or updated research or statistics to reinforce the continuation of the design—or changes to it. Once you collect and organize all the information and updates, go ahead and rewrite the proposal. Take care to edit some of the sentences where you don't change the information. This should help the material feel fresh and intentional to the reader, not too familiar and staid. It is difficult to keep the tone and flow balanced throughout with spot editing, so leave time to set aside this proposal, too, and then reread with fresh eyes and ears.

Finishing Up

You are nearly done. Whatever your submittal format, it's time to review the materials you've created before you press the submit button. Here's a list of basics for the end of the proposal process.

- Remember to remove the parking lot section if you created one; save it as its own document for other projects, if you want it.
- If there is no one to proof your materials, do it yourself as methodically as possible. You have two options: wait a day or two to proof before submitting, and/or proof by reading each sentence but starting from the end of the document. The reverse order of text forces you to be more attentive to catch the meaning, and you are much more likely to catch mistakes as you work through the words.
- Check the formatting: Is it consistent throughout the document? Is it helpful or confusing? Does it keep to the margin and page range? Is the font correct?
- Gather all the attachment materials in one place, preferably their permanent spot on your system so that you do not need to do extra filing once the proposal has been submitted. At that point, you will want a break and a bit of a celebration, not another filing chore. This will make it more efficient to upload or attach the files, and it will help ensure you include them all.
- Take a break; then sit down for a final review before submittal. Do not hurry as you submit, or you may make a silly mistake at the last stressed or tired moment.
- Now you can celebrate.

Now let's get more specific about individual writing projects by looking at letters of inquiry, sometimes called letters of interest, and concept letters, sometimes called concept papers. No matter what their names, these are submittals that are preliminaries to a potential grant application. There's no guarantee you'll be invited to apply for a grant, but you do get a chance to put your cause in front of the funder and to possibly collect some feedback. Whatever the result, they are valuable for clarifying the design, value, and result of a project or program.

THE PROCESS OF WRITING AND REWRITING

For a glimpse into the writing process, here are three examples of the evolution of first-paragraph openings in letters of inquiry. Each has one or two rewrites. You can see how sentence structure improves, whether the text is longer or shorter, and where there is greater clarity and specificity in the final versions compared to the first ones.

The Charles Lawrence House
Version 1
The basement at Charles Lawrence House has six inches of water in it at high tide—that's twice a day, every day; more with a king tide. Historically this seaside location was a benefit; with sea level rise and coastal flooding it is no longer an advantage for this, the home of the region's most celebrated ship captain. It is the modern-day home of the largest intact collection of colonial-era maps and navigational equipment on the East Coast—a treasure trove of colonial-era trade history. It faces a future unable to care for the collection as moisture threatens the structure and requires greater intervention to produce climate conditions for paper and metal artifacts vulnerable to salt and moisture.

Version 2
The basement of the Charles Lawrence House has six inches of water in it at high tide—that's twice a day, every day; more with a king tide (greater because of the full moon). Historically this seaside location was a benefit; with sea level rise and coastal flooding it is no longer an advantage for this 1785 wooden historic structure. It faces a future unable to care for the collection as moisture threatens the structure and requires greater intervention to produce climate conditions for paper and metal artifacts vulnerable to salt and moisture. The house was built for the

region's most celebrated ship captain, and now houses the largest intact collection of colonial-era navigational charts and equipment on the East Coast as a tool for studying and interpreting colonial-era trade history.

The most appropriate protection for paper and metal artifacts vulnerable to salt and moisture is passive climate control through individual cases, and buffered storage in purpose-built files. Though removing these artifacts also would protect them, it would separate them from the story of how they were used, who used them, and why.

Version 3

The basement of the Charles Lawrence House has six inches of water in it at high tide—that's twice a day, every day; more with a king tide (more extreme with a full moon). Historically this seaside location was a benefit, but with sea level rise and coastal flooding the location is no longer an advantage for this 1785 wooden historic structure. The house was built for the region's most celebrated ship captain and now houses the largest intact collection of colonial-era navigational charts and equipment on the East Coast. They are an invaluable resource for studying and interpreting colonial-era trade history. The Lawrence House faces a future unable to care for the collection as moisture threatens the structure and requires greater intervention to produce climate conditions for paper and metal artifacts vulnerable to salt and moisture.

We are grateful that the Johnson Foundation has invited a concept letter from the Lawrence House Society in support of a $25,000 project to safely house the collection while assessing long-term options for protecting the Charles Lawrence House. The most appropriate protection for these paper and metal artifacts vulnerable to salt and moisture is passive climate control through individual cases, and buffered storage in purpose-built files. Though we could also protect these artifacts by storing them elsewhere, that move would isolate them from their story: how exploration, travel, and commerce thrived in a time of oceanic voyages based on wind power and celestial navigation, connecting countries and building empires when travel entailed greater risk, expense, and time.

The Johnstown Center
Version 1

Thank you for the invitation to submit a concept paper on behalf of the Johnstown Center's annual exhibit. Our rural community has traditionally been home to Native Americans, European immigrants, and Americans who migrated here from the eastern colonies. This mix of residents has
(continued)

THE PROCESS OF WRITING AND REWRITING *(continued)*

a varied history of interactions, and recent discussions have raised the interest in sharing cultural stories.

Version 2
Thank you, Ms. Peale, for the invitation to submit a concept paper on behalf of the Johnstown Center's annual exhibit. This fall and winter, several families spent months participating in the Dakota Access Pipeline protests, and many in our community contributed funds and supplies to support the effort. While our rural community has a historical mix of Native Americans, European immigrants, and American residents who migrated here from the eastern colonies, our exhibits have always focused on individual histories. The pipeline discussions have raised interest in sharing the overlap of experience rather than isolated histories. This exhibit on our community's continuing experience with the pipeline protests provides a special opportunity to create an exhibit with multiple stories, one that is embedded in today's experience with connections to the past, not one solely focused on the past.

Petersen Exhibit
Version 1
When Sarah Petersen began drawing the landscape around her, she had no expectation of becoming the celebrated artist we now know her to be. Fifty-seven of her paintings are being brought together for the first time, but that's not what is so special about this exhibit. Now rather than seeing them solely for their art, and as the story of a woman making a name for herself in the art world, environmentalists and planners recognize them for their value in understanding the landscape of south central Indiana, and the degree of change over the last one hundred years. They illustrate how man has changed the land, and how those changes have affected man's built environment in unexpected ways: the dams and redirecting of the river, construction in flood plains, and finally, the withdrawal of water for city expansion.

Version 2
When Sarah Petersen began drawing the landscape around her, she had no expectation of becoming the celebrated artist we now know her to be. Fifty-seven of her paintings are being brought together for the first time, but that's not what is so special about this exhibit. Now rather than seeing them solely for their art, and as the story of a woman making a name for

herself in the art world, environmentalists and planners recognize them for their value in understanding the landscape of south central Indiana, and how those changes contributed to the urban challenges of water shortages and, ironically, flooding we face one hundred years later. The Grand Coulee Art Museum would like to be invited to apply for $50,000 to support the design and installation of the exhibit, for display June 1 through December 31. We expect a significant portion of the exhibit to travel to at least three additional locations in the coming years.

Note: The following sentence is still valuable, but it should appear later on in the letter or be saved for the full proposal depending upon space: "They illustrate how man has changed the land, and how those changes have affected man's built environment in unexpected ways: the dams and redirection of the river, construction in flood plains, and, finally, the withdrawal of water for city expansion."

Version 3
When Sarah Petersen began drawing the landscape around her, she likely did not expect to become the celebrated artist we now know her to be. Fifty-seven of her paintings are being brought together for the first time, but that's not what is so special about this exhibit. Rather than solely as art, or the story of a woman making a name for herself in the nineteenth-century art world, now environmentalists and planners recognize them as valuable records of the historic landscape of south central Indiana, and how man-made changes contributed to the urban challenges of water shortages and, ironically, flooding we face 130 years later. The Grand Coulee Art Museum would like to be invited to apply for $50,000 to support the design and installation of the exhibit for display June 1 through December 31. We expect twenty to thirty images to travel to state art museums and two other regional art museums in the subsequent two years.

NOTE

1. Elizabeth Wylie, email with the author, September 18, 2017.

CHAPTER 7

Which Is It?
A Letter of Inquiry/Interest or a Concept Letter/Paper?

"Seriously? An LOI?"

Every once in a while, your tired, overworked self may surface, and you'll hear this voice in your head: "Am I going to have to write these people twice to get a grant?!"

Ignore that voice. Shut it down. Instead, trust that the funder's request for a concept letter or concept paper, or a letter of inquiry or letter of interest (that LOI you exclaimed about), is to your benefit.

Whatever the funder specifies is a good thing, because these instructions improve your chances of getting to "yes," and they reduce the guesswork of the most appropriate approach and materials for the request. Starting with a concept letter or paper and letter of interest or inquiry allows the foundation staff to review the potential applicants, identify those that are the most interesting and likely to be competitive, and invite the organizations to submit a full proposal for funding. This helps the staff or the volunteer board members easily process the great volume of requests they receive. The basic questions and summary responses mean fewer pages of material for them to read *and* for you to prepare. They have your interests in mind, too. They hope to prevent you from spending your limited time on a proposal unlikely to be successful. If they feel that the alignment between their interests and your project is strong, that the project need is compelling, and that you are the appropriate organization to work with, then they will ask for full details in a full proposal.

THE FORMAT

If the differences among LOIs and a concept letter or paper seem vague, it is because there is no agreed-upon difference to begin with. Funders use the term they feel is the most appropriate and provide the instructions to support it. Let's simplify this process by referring to all these preliminary letters or papers as LOIs and by focusing on how to use them to everyone's advantage.

The LOI is a condensed version of a full application. There are two formats: text documents and online forms. The text documents can be a set of prompt questions from the funder, if they are provided, or your own structure. The online form will likely have drop-down menus for describing the audience and choosing the program category; blanks for filling in the organizational name and address, request amounts, and institutional budgets; and a series of program and organizational answer boxes associated with each question. Though these forms are technically awkward and extremely inelegant for writing, they *do* focus your responses.

Fill-In Forms

If the donor provides a form for the letter, it will be either one to download, fill in, and send by email or one to fill in and submit through the foundation's portal. The good news about being presented with a form is that it clearly indicates what to include and how much space to use; the bad news is that it is harder to make the text read well.

For those forms that you download and email, it is easiest and safest to save it electronically to your computer, answer the questions and fill in the blanks, and then save and attach it to an email with a message like the ones described above. For those that are a fill-in form accessed and submitted through the foundation's portal, it can feel quite awkward to develop the text, so there are some tips for the process below.

Access to the online form is usually through a "To Apply" button on the main website. You often must register your email address and password, submit your institution's vital information to establish your institution's eligibility to apply, and also create your record in the foundation's database. If and when you submit material again, whether as a full proposal, a report, or a new LOI, you will use this same access point.

For either form, text or online, your best, smoothest writing will be done offline. Sometimes there is a way to save the form's question text to your computer to use as a draft for formatting your response. If there is not an easy way to save the package, as they call the all-online answer form, then take the time to re-create it in a word-processing format, whether by copying and pasting the text or retyping it. Then you can write and edit your answers before cutting and pasting them into the all-online form for submittal.

Your letter will be strongest, in both formats, if it flows smoothly and logically from one question to the next. "Do not answer as if you are being interrogated," says Frances Phillips of the Walter and Elise Haas Fund. The grants officer is familiar with the questions and has many LOIs to work through; he or she may well skim the material looking for the story and mental image that helps tie it together and make it memorable among the sea of applications.[1] By using the questions to organize your words, you can still write as if the questions were missing and this were part of the natural flow of a text document.

The questions may seem redundant; this likely reflects some in-house organizational needs, so do not let it stymie you. Take care to double check the length of your answers. Often the online form counts spaces and characters differently from your word-processing document. You may find the counts in the form are higher than in your word-processing document. Just keep editing and pasting until you find the best approach. The availability of this technology as easy access for applicants, and for funders to sort and locate applications, has meant that the technology rather than design drives this format. The portal is simply a tool for working with the funder; it is not an attempt to make the process intentionally challenging. With practice, you will learn how to meet the criteria of the format while retaining the distinctive character of your institution and your project.

The online process usually has a formal "submit" button and a tracking system that lets you know your LOI has been received. It saves a copy for you and usually allows you to save and print the entire form. If you are invited to submit a proposal, the process will use this same portal, so take care to record your login information now!

Text Formats

When the requested form is for a text document to be emailed to the program officer as an attachment, make it a three-page letter, or a two-page statement with a one-page cover letter. Prepare it using an electronic version of your letterhead; then format the material as a letter, with a date and salutation to open and a closing signature. If the funder gives you the sections that organize your response, then use bold titles for each narrative section to simplify their reading and ensure that you address all the requested topics. If the funder does not provide a specific format, try the approach described below. In either case, please use a 12-point font and one-inch margins for comfortable reading and possible note-taking by the reader.

Open with an introduction that names the problem and the solution, the amount of money you would like to request, and what previous contact you've had with the funder. If you have spoken to a program officer and/or been invited to apply, then say so right away. The reader will know immediately that you have proceeded to this stage thoughtfully, and with good reason. If you have not had contact with the funder, explain that you have read the giving guidelines and visited the website to understand their giving interests.

Then, in the subsequent sections, with almost always more than one paragraph per section, explain:

- the story, mission, and audience for your museum
- the need (problem or opportunity, and underlying causes or issues)
- how you came to the solution
- the solution and what is needed to deliver it
- why you are best suited to deliver this solution

If any of these sections stump you, consider two things: either you do not yet fully understand the challenge or you are not yet well prepared to address it. Both conundrums indicate a need to step back and work through the understanding of the problem and the design of the project before applying for support. That is part of grant readiness. Getting there may mean more research, more observation of others working on this issue, or more conversations with the community and perhaps even with the funder. All of this effort will build strength into your work and prepare you for the LOI later. Remember, a deadline is not a reason for an LOI—or a grant—but an awesome project is.

The most important part of the entire message is the intersection of their money with your solution to a demonstrated need. Without that story, the rest is irrelevant. In good, engaging narrative form, deliver that message with foreshadowing in the opening paragraph and a dénouement in the last. You can use these components to construct answers to the questions in any online form as well, although they may appear in a different sequence. Rely on powerful facts and/or a powerful story to make a memorable, compelling case. Illustrate how you thoughtfully approached the design of the solution based on needs, best practice, and experience. Then explain the difference your solution makes by describing it as a result of the methods you use or the approach you take. Conclude with why you are particularly suited to provide this valuable solution.

OPERATING SUPPORT LOIs

What do you write about if your LOI is for a general operating support (GOS) rather than a community-directed need? The focus is your organization, but it's still about the difference the organization makes, and all the issues or problems it addresses. In that case, describe your intentions for the next year or two, demonstrating how they align with institutional planning and represent a natural progression of improved community service. For example, if you have completed some assessment, explain how and why this grant would help you implement recommendations. What will these changes help you do? If you have completed a phase of your strategic plan and are about to renew the plan, explain how this support provides the staff time and focus to do so.

If you merely state that these funds will allow you to conduct evaluations, scale a project, or provide professional development, then your request is likely to be too self-serving, too limited, to attract support. If you describe how the evaluations allow you to improve school program alignment with teacher needs; or how scaling the project allows you to reach the third, fourth, and fifth grades with iterative learning; or how professional development will improve your staff's ability to deal with difficult questions and contentious topics prevalent in local current events, then this tells the funder that you identify your internal needs based on audience needs and the desire to improve your performance. The funder can now see how a grant benefits you and your audience, rather than your museum alone.

For example, it is far more effective to introduce your museum with more of a story about its responsiveness to current needs. You could state that the mission has evolved over the decades from a historic association in the nineteenth century to an active community-focused center that for the last decade has been a showcase for community stories and a platform for community discussion. This demonstrates longevity and adaptability while introducing the case for the need and for your commitment to addressing it.

Next, take care to make sure your reader quickly feels confident that you have the perspective and presence to address this problem and are doing so with an audience that it, too, is interested in. Add a sentence about whom you serve, first generally, and then specifically, because of this situation. For example, "While the Minnesota immigrant community feels threatened by current politics, and the nonimmigrant community wonders how to react to the current situation, the historical association is ideally suited to provide facts and individual stories reflecting the experience of past immigrants to the Twin Cities, such as the Scandinavians and the Germans, and provide a setting for illustrating and discussing present-day experiences of the Hmong and Somalis." What matters about the organization's history is that you can tie it to the design of the project at hand while demonstrating that it has the capability to deliver a thoughtful solution. Save the detailed history for the proposal, and move instead from the scene you have just set to how your proposed work addresses the needs of the community and why you know this is a valuable approach.

If you have received money from this funder before, mention it and the results of that grant either quite briefly in the opening paragraph or near the end of the letter.[2] If the grant is completed, you should have submitted the report before beginning this letter. If you can provide a summary of the proposed project in a statement approximating a 140-character tweet, you will leave a lasting impression.[3] You may close with a flourishing paragraph that includes your museum's success in serving an appropriate audience, and how the foundation's support amplifies that good work.

JUST THREE PAGES? ARE THEY SERIOUS?

There's that incredulous voice again. I can hear you thinking, "Three pages? I have to plan the whole program and practically write the whole proposal before I have the answers for this, and then I have to cut it all back?!" Yes, you do. To attract the funder's attention, something they choose to give you and do not *have* to give you, you must present your best work, and that requires quality research and planning. It also means that you will be able to easily answer any questions if a program officer inquires, and you will quickly turn around a full proposal once invited. You may find that the subsequent chapters on designing proposals and using logic models will help you get ready to write the LOI.

The grant process is predicated not on hope but on commitment. Do not submit a project that you *hope* will interest them; submit one you're committed to and believe the funder will commit to as well.

Submitting the Text Letter

If this is a text document to be sent by email, then in your email message do the following:

- explain that your organization is submitting a letter of inquiry
- name the program and category
- mention whether this is your first inquiry or whether you have worked with the funder before
- add something to pique interest and plant your letter firmly in the reader's mind for later
- explain that you have attached the letter of inquiry, plus any requested materials, such as the tax-exemption letter from the IRS, and institutional and program budget information
- provide your phone contact information for questions or further discussion

That email message might look like this:

Hello Ms. Johnson.

I am submitting this Letter of Inquiry on behalf of the Lawrence County Museum and Science Center. Thank you for speaking with me last month about the General Operating Support program at the Lawrence Community Foundation, and for encouraging this approach. I have attached the inquiry letter, our tax letter, and budget information.

We look forward to hearing from you. You may reach me at 978-505-4515 if you have questions or are interested in further discussion.

Thank you for your consideration.

Sincerely,

Sarah Sutton

Grants Officer

It could also look like this—slightly more conversational and sufficiently engaging to remain distinctive in the reader's mind in the future, and only fourteen words longer:

Good morning, Ms. Johnson.

I am submitting this Letter of Inquiry from the Lawrence County Museum and Science Center. Thank you for the time last month to discuss the General Operating Support program at the Lawrence Community Foundation, and for encouraging this approach. It is so important that our staff have dedicated research and planning time, through such a grant, to design and test the citizen science modules requested by the county schools as part of their new environmental curriculum.

I have attached the inquiry letter, our tax letter, and budget information. If you have questions or would like to talk more, I am at 978-505-4515 or sarah@LCMS.org.

Thank you for your consideration,

Sarah Sutton

Grants Officer

That's it. All your efforts and descriptive information should go into the letter. Since the LOI will be separated from this email, anything you put in the email would have to be repeated in the main letter anyway.

FOLLOW-UP

If this was a free-form letter and you concluded with a message indicating that you would call the funder (common but not recommended), then do call and ask to schedule a chance to speak with a program officer. If you are lucky, then you will be able to speak to one right away, so be ready to. If you submitted a form and the website does not indicate when you will receive a response, it is reasonable to call the funder for an update three weeks after submittal if you have not had a response.[4] The delay is likely that the funder is waiting to collect enough letters before setting a time to sort through them all, or simply returning from travel or addressing other internal deadlines. If the website indicates when you will hear, please wait until after that date to contact the funder.

What happens if they say yes? Celebrate! Send an email back saying "thank you" for the invitation for a full proposal. Then help your director or board chair write a brief note indicating your plan to apply and thanking them for the invitation. Now it's time to put all your hard work into the full court press!

NOTES

1. Frances Phillips, "Crafting a Competitive LOI," webinar, Foundation Center training event, GrantSpace, May 24, 2016.

2. Goodwin Deacon and Ken Ristine, *Grantsmanship for the Genius: A Master Grantwriter and a Veteran Funder Reveal the Keys to Winning Grants* (Nashville, TN: For the Genius Press, 2016), 236.

3. Phillips, "Competitive LOI."

4. Phillips, "Competitive LOI."

CHAPTER 8

Building and Submitting
the Proposal Package

Congratulations! You earned an invitation to submit a full proposal!

Shoot! Now you have to recall the whole project and write it all down, only in more detail.

The good news is that all the earlier planning and design has prepared you for this. So, check the proposal's due date. Then read and reread the guidelines, and note what attachments you will need. Then review the budget notes you saved. Next, retrieve the LOI you submitted and begin adding back what you had wanted to say in the first version, following the proposal instructions. Simple, right? Only until you get to the hardest part about proposal writing: knowing what information to put in and what to leave out. Try to keep it simple by following the guidelines for content and organization, keeping the content and language clear, and telling a story.

If you're asking for general operating support (GOS) versus support for a project or program grant, look at the content as a macro description rather than a micro one. The GOS support, the macro approach, is the full version of your mission-based work and all the support activities for that work. Program and project support is for more micro or specific aspects inside that larger package. Two other distinguishing features between the two proposal types are time frame and outcomes. GOS is money to use as you wish during a fiscal year for running your organization. Program and project money is for specific activities during a specific time frame that may or may not coincide with a fiscal year. Because GOS is general and not tied to a specific activity, there are no direct outcomes related to it, but rather general ones associated with fulfilling your institutional mission appropriately.

Fortunately, whether you're writing a GOS proposal or project proposal, the funder usually provides the questions and often extra prompts for the information that help you choose what to include in the response. Likely somewhere they describe criteria for evaluating your proposal, either question by question or overall.

NARRATIVE MATERIAL

If the proposal format is primarily a text document to be attached to an email or submitted through a portal as a Word or other document, the funder will usually provide an outline. If they do not, then go ahead and use this one, or something close to it. Usually funders use these categories in varying order:

- introduction
- audience
- programs
- resources
- this request
- institutional history
- staff and board
- challenges and opportunities

Introduction

The reader will want to know when the organization was established, but not necessarily by whom unless that legacy is an important part of your current format. Provide your mission, and likely a one-sentence review of its evolution to this point. Note the location and size of your organization, the size of the budget, number of staff, and how many people you reach each year. Then briefly introduce the request. You can launch into more detail in each section of the proposal format provided by the funder.

Audience

This is about whom you will serve in the project and how many. If you're asking for support for a program, this is easy: your audience is the group of people you plan to attract to the project. If it's a building project, then it's all the people who will experience the building in the future. If you're asking for support for a collections project, then this is a little more complex: the audience is who will benefit from access to the collections in the future.

Programs

Here you have to decide how many programs to describe. If you have many, or a wide variety, then you may opt to list a number of them in a sentence, or to bullet major ones with a description of each using only a few words. Then you can elaborate on those that demonstrate capacity, or demand, for the project that is the subject of the application.

Resources

This includes the buildings, physical spaces, talent, and connections to people and organizations that help you do your work. This includes your collections. Depending upon space in the document, use broad terms that describe the collections, and then provide a few highlighted examples that reinforce your alignment with the funder or your appeal to the public. If your application is about a program, then the space for hosting it is a critical component.

This Request

This, of course, is the most important part: the what, where, when, and how. Don't forget to include how much the project costs and how much you're asking for. The funder will give you specific guidelines here, and the bulk of your proposal will be making this case.

Institutional History

This helps the funder understand how you came about, how you've evolved. A paragraph or two will be enough.

Please do not open your organizational description with "Founded in 1873, the Maui County Historical Society's mission is . . ." The founding date and the mission are not intimately related to each other and do not belong in the same sentence. Try this: *The Maui Historical Society's mission is [fill in the blank]. Since 1873, volunteers and professional staff have collected and interpreted the prehistoric and historic material that tell the island's story. Each year three exhibits circulate among the two historic sites and one gallery open to the public. Fifty-nine thousand guests, 75 percent locals, participate in programs and visit the exhibits and collection each year. The Native Hawaiian cultural programs are our most popular, and the source of the society's reputation as a valuable community partner in protecting and perpetuating Maui heritage.*

Staff and Board

The basics will do here: how many of them, their backgrounds and experience, and what skills and other value they bring you. For the board, this may just be a list with affiliations. For the staff, it's a running list with a phrase or two about specific skills or talents and previous related experience.

Challenges and Opportunities

The funder needs to know you will be honest and fair with them; this is where you prove it. They need to know that you must or can do what is important to the institution's continued ability to fulfill its mission. Take a few sentences to allude to what has led to this request, even if it was challenging, and how completing this project will move the institution forward.

WHEN YOU'RE REUSING A PROPOSAL

Caution: When reusing material for a proposal, allow for the process to take more effort and rewriting than you or others expect. Yes, the writing and editing process will be shorter than if you started from scratch, but there is no such thing as "boilerplate," as some describe the sections of text they consider reusable over and over again. The material must be fresh and well aligned for the funder's interests. You *will* be able to reuse some of the material, but the wording, tone, and details must be refreshed each time. The funder will be able to tell if you wrote this especially for them or took shortcuts by reusing material carelessly. Reviewers are very sensitive to careless reuse of text and materials in a proposal.

The organizational description will need updating as you add a program or note that the organization or its activities are a year older than in last year's version. You should include any major changes, such as new staff and leadership volunteers, acquiring or renovating a building, acquiring an important collections item or items, or winning an award or other valuable recognition. Your descriptive data will need updating as well: audience types and sizes, annual budget total, staff and volunteer numbers, and the names of highlight events from the year, such as exhibits, special speakers, or a new partnership. If you have reviewed your mission and/or updated it, take the time to mention this change and make the case for relevance to the organization's trajectory and contemporary needs and value. This is another opportunity in the proposal to remind your readers why you matter and the difference you make.

FORMATTING

For online fill-in forms where you may, depending upon the software, have much less formatting ability, at a minimum you should review the material you paste into the fill-in box. Pasting your text into their program often produces unexpected formatting. Please make sure there are spaces between a period and the beginning of the next sentence, as well as between paragraphs, and that any bullets are spaced properly.

BULLETS, BOLDING, AND BOXES

When your narrative is a document you upload instead of dropping it into a box, you can be more creative and engaging than within the confines of an online fill-in form. The growth of electronic media delivery is changing the way many expect to read and consume information. Many of your reviewers have adapted to become information consumers primarily through multimedia formats. Though they may be primed for this approach, the accepted proposal format is not yet multimedia. So, though you wouldn't design a proposal as a web page or a blog post, you can include aspects learned from these sites for successful reader engagement.

Imagine websites you respond to positively: you see an engaging or arresting image; white space and a strong-contrast typeface; no jumbled typefaces or hues; no tightly formatted text and not too many bullets or boxes, but some. To translate this to your documents, this means:

- creating white space on each page (for resting the reader's eyes and brain)
- using a few images effectively (to convey more information than you can in the text, and to make your message and proposal more memorable)
- shaping the formatting to guide the reader's understanding (by clearly illustrating that you have addressed all the categories; conserve the reader's energy for continuing easily, section by section, by using boldface for signaling progress)

PHOTOGRAPHS

You likely cannot add photographs in a fill-in form online, but if you are allowed to attach additional documents, consider attaching one with a few well-captioned photographs. Whether part of an attachment or embedded in the proposal, the photographs should

- relate directly to adjacent text
- convey either energy or detail that text space does not allow
- have brief captions (the font size can be a bit smaller than the main text, but not too small)
- be so visually effective that they anchor your proposal in the readers' minds

In a successful application to NEH for Sustaining Cultural Heritage Collections, Dumbarton House included images of dolls and tableware stored inside dressers—all collections items—to make the case for increasing storage capacity and upgrading environmental conditions. You should aim to fit two, preferably three, photographs into a seven-page proposal. This will strengthen your connection to the reader without giving up too much text space or making the proposal look like a website.

ONLINE SUBMITTALS

As we reviewed in chapter 7, electronic submission is nearly universal for private funders. It can be as simple as an email with an attachment you've completed by downloading a form from the funder's website and filling it out. More likely you will find yourself following a "To Apply" link from the funder website to a hosted online program that provides the instructions and all the fill-in portions of the grant proposal and designated places for uploading documents. That online proposal format is the focus of this section.

The Portal

The online format for submitting proposals, the portal, may be hosted by the funder or by an organization that manages the portal and supports the grants process for the funder. Sometimes multiple funders use a single grant management organization's portal. When you log in, you will be taken to the funder's application screen. You may see a history of your applications to that funder and to other funders you've applied to who use the same portal. There will be a "Start a New Proposal" link for the specific funder. Usually this takes you to a checkbox link to make sure you are connected to the right applicant data already in the portal. This page has very basic information associated with your organization, such as institutional name and address and contact name and email. From there the funder's application form will likely take you through a series of other pages:

- *Institutional Information*: This will likely be your institution's name and address again, its Tax ID or Employer Identification Number, date of origin, and mission statement. It will also ask again for institutional contact information, this time for the president or CEO and the contact for this proposal. It likely will ask for the number of staff and volunteers and a fill-in list of your board members. Often the portal will store this kind of information so you can edit it each time instead of adding each name for every application.

- *Proposal Information*: This is usually the request amount and time frame, audience demographics, and geographical information such as counties, regions, or states.
- *Request Information*: This is where you describe your project purpose, activities, format, and partners.
- *Goals and Objectives*: This will likely be a full page of sections to check, edit, or add to.
- *Financial Information*: This is where you will enter some totals and then attach documents such as the program and institutional budgets, and likely an audited financial statement and/or a Form 990.

The material you already entered in your LOI may not populate the application, but you can access the LOI for reference. As you work through the proposal, you can usually save your content and work on different parts of different pages. You can even return to a draft if you need to close out and return later or another day.

As with the LOI online format, you want to remember to tell a story, just with more detail. You might want to prepare the whole thing offline and read it to see whether it flows nicely. When you have the final version, cut and paste each answer into its box. Be careful of the character count, if they register one. Some portals count spaces and new lines as characters; others do not. You might type something in Word and count the characters only to find that the portal's program counts the same text with more characters and truncates your answer. The reader can only judge what they see, so make sure they see all that you want them to see.

If you have any attachments, be sure to check the formatting on documents you convert to pdf format for submittal. That conversion can mean unexpected symbols in document titles and text and different spacing leading to more pages in your document. Take care not to let the conversion process put your document over the page limit. The funder likely won't accept the excuse. When it's time to submit, and you've uploaded everything and reread your text to be sure it fits the portal format requirements, you'll select "Check Application." This is not foolproof, but it often catches a missed document or an overlooked drop-down menu. After you submit, capture the electronic copy for your files.

Grants.gov

Just as a portal may provide access for applications to many funders, the federal online portal, grants.gov, provides access to multiple agencies' proposals. The portal has its own set of instructions for users, and the funding agencies have their own set of proposal guidelines for applicants as they prepare materials to submit through the portal. Grants.gov is visually quite different from the private foundation portals. It also has a few levels of authentication to work through, but you have access to knowledgeable twenty-four-hour assistance by phone if you need it. That's a huge bonus when you're struggling to gain access or something is not loading properly. Some federal agencies may have letters of intent that you submit this way, but mostly you will use the portal for full applications to NEH, IMLS, the National Science Foundation, and the National Endowment for the Arts. When you apply for that first IMLS grant or that first NEH Preservation Access grant, this is where you go. Start by identifying your organization's DUNS number, the Dun & Bradstreet (D&B) identifier. You likely have one, but you need to track it down first. If you don't know, the D&B website will help you locate it. Use it for registering with grants.gov. The process takes from a few days to a couple of weeks, so be sure to allow enough time. This is not something you do during submittal week.

Once the organization is registered, you'll have to register at least two people for submitting proposals. One will be the E-Biz point of contact—the financial contact; the other is the Authorized Organization Representative (AOR). If you have only one staff member, the director is the E-Biz and the board chair the AOR. If you have more staff than one, then you can assign the roles appropriately. You may have more than one AOR for an organization, but not more than one E-Biz point of contact. This is so that in a larger organization, more than one department can be working on and submitting applications. You can also make a consultant or contractor an AOR. The AORs are able to work in Workspace, the name of the portal section for the grant opportunity (more on that below). Here is an overview of the application process and a few tips on making the process work well for you, but the online instructions for both grants.gov and the agencies are the final word on how to complete the process.

> The instructions for both DUNS and grants.gov are available on the grants.gov website. The website gives you full instructions for using it, and the funder will have instructions for how to prepare your proposal. If you have questions about the website, call the grants.gov helpline. If you have questions about the material to put into the proposal, call the funder.

You can start using this portal as soon as the application becomes available. This is usually about six to eight weeks before the application deadline. Up until then you can access an archived version of the previous year's guidelines so that you can begin planning. This has some risk because the guidelines, expectations, and preferences do tend to change somewhat at least every other year. If you are concerned about potential changes, then monitor the webinars and news reports online for notices, and speak to a program officer to keep up with expected changes. Once the application goes live, you can capture the Catalog of Federal Domestic Assistance (CFDA) number from the program website, or by searching grants.gov using the agency name and the application name to find the CFDA number. With that you can gain access to the instructions and set up Workspace.

On the entry page for Workspace you will find instructions and tutorials on using it to streamline the completion and submittal process. It will ask you to identify the "owner" of the Workspace and to set the roles of others using it. The tutorials will show you how to do this, and also how to access the instructions and forms you will need for the application package. Some forms will be web pages with blanks to fill in and drop-down menus to complete; others will have spaces for uploading pdf documents from your own computer. The first form is a simple fill-in SF-424 that every agency uses. Consider the SF-424 the informational cover sheet. It has excellent instructions to help you complete it. It asks for information on the project contact, the audience, the type of institution (museum, higher education, hospital, etc.), beginning and end dates, and information on your political district. It will not be prepopulated no matter how many times you use it, so save a copy on your computer to use as a shortcut for filling it out for the next proposal.

One of the online forms is designated for uploading all your attachments:

- often an abstract
- definitely the proposal
- the budget
- a document of collected staff bios
- another for consultant bios with commitment letters and agreements
- any supporting materials, such as:
  - condition or historical assessments
  - relevant legal announcements or commitments
- supplementary documents such as photos, maps, or illustrations

When you finish a form as an AOR and do not want others to make changes to it, you can lock that document by clicking on the lock symbol. Otherwise, leave it unlocked for your team members to help you by adding specific information.

The agency's application instructions will tell you which materials to create, in what format, how to name them, and the order in which to attach them. It is different for each, so when you read the instructions, take special note of this section. That means you may write the whole proposal by following the questions in the narrative and think you are ready for an upload and submittal, only to find you're missing a document that is listed as an attachment and not part of the narrative. For example, with IMLS you will be asked to provide a separate summary of the organization's history as a one-page attachment. Sometimes there is room for letters of support. Please do not go overboard here; one or two strategic selections will do. You do not want to overwhelm the readers. Use a letter from a legislator if that is provided as an example; if it isn't provided, then it is not appropriate, politically. Choose, instead,

- a peer to write a short statement for you about the importance of the topic or your ability to fulfill your project goals
- a potential beneficiary with knowledge of your organization
- an institutional governing agency, such as:
  - a tribal leader or the council
  - your parent organization or the fiscal agent
  - your municipal parent if a department of a town, city, or county

That's why it's so important to search for the funder's Application Checklist: it's a good way to be sure you can collect the best documents in time for submittal.

Using Workspace

This is a simple, easy way to see and complete all the components of the grant application. The advantage is that the portal allows other members of the project team, or staff with access to particular types of material, to directly contribute to the proposal—either by adding information to the web forms or by uploading pdf attachments—and then others can see what has already been completed. This means that the financial officer can upload a budget total and the budget form if you're not the one to do it, or that the curator can upload a conservation assessment under "supplemental documents" without sending it to you to upload. You'll be able to see that it's been added, and check it, too. This also means two of you can be looking at the material in the portal when you're doing the final submittal process. That way, two sets of eyes can confirm the submission. This is excellent for catching typos, mistakes, and oversights.

The Upload

When it's time to submit a complex proposal such as a state or federal application, I recommend you set aside some time to do so deliberately. Workspace makes this simpler, but any complex application deserves quiet attention so you can be sure you have completed all the forms and are ready to attach all the appropriate documents in the correct format and with requested file names. It's important to check each one before you release it. It is too easy to skip something during the preparation process, thinking you'll complete it later, and too easy to overlook an important section of the fill-in form when you just couldn't find the right number for that blank! If you leave time to check and submit the application, then you also have the time to fix any last-minute surprises. It's worth having someone else look at the documents with you as you carefully check and/or include them during the final submittal. The process will eliminate any worries you have about the correctness or completion of your application, and that will be comforting as you wait to hear, for sure.

WHY SO MANY PROPOSALS ARE SUBMITTED JUST IN TIME

Even with a good deal of lead time, most proposals are submitted on the due date or just a few days before. This is because we are human. We work on the most urgent issues first, taking the others in chronological order. However, just-in-time submittals are very stressful for the submitter and their helpers. Often just-in-time submittals are not thoroughly prepared, thoroughly reviewed, or professionally finished. There are various tricks to reduce the likelihood of this happening. Some people tell their staff the deadline is actually earlier than it really is (though I suspect the word gets out); some know the material will come together late, so they block off the week before the proposal due date and put off all other work at that time. Some get very good at creating a preparation schedule with flexibility built into it and nudge all helpers to keep to that schedule. Whatever approach you take, keep reminding contributors and helpers that the deadline is looming and you cannot do your work well unless they do theirs in a timely manner. If you are concerned that you may miss the deadline and suffer repercussions, document the dates you receive necessary materials so that you have an internal paper trail to explain the challenge of the process, protect yourself, and act as a discussion document that leads to more intentional team planning in the future.

For many, this shepherding is the most frustrating part of the process. The good news is that the online portals often give you a path to uploading and completing portions of the proposal as you are able, so that you have less material to rush into the submittal format in the last days. In the absence of a shared portal, if you have the wherewithal to create such an internal system of information submittal—even a simple form that outlines sections, staff responsible, and due date—you can at least shape the process to make the final submittal easier. Once it's finally in, take a moment to celebrate a completed project and the potential for a grant to move you forward. Congratulations!

CHAPTER 9

After It's In!

Now all you have to do is wait for three to nine months until the awards date. Well, no. You have two more responsibilities: tidying the information related to the application and contacting the funder if something important comes up.

MORE RECORD-KEEPING

I know you think you will never forget this grant application—who it's to, for how much, and when you'll hear. But you will forget. Once you move on to the next application, the older one will be pushed right out of your brain. Don't let that happen until you've done some housekeeping. Chapter 3 addresses donor records, and now you'll need to add donor contact activities to them. So, create a simple process to capture information, now, that can be reliably accessed later. First, record the application date, request amount, purpose, and funder in either your database or a spreadsheet. Choose whatever format is available to you—financially and technologically. Adapt it as much as possible to your own preferences, making it easy to use for you and others who might access it without you. Take a moment to organize it so you can sort it by due dates, notice dates, and projects. This will make it easier to check it quickly to see what proposals are due and which award announcements to look for in the next quarter, and then to organize your lists of prospects and donors. Be sure that this document or system includes the request amount, the award amount (they may be different), and a Yes/No column for whether you got the grant. These last three make it easy to list the amount of money and grants pursued and how much you received. You'll use that when you evaluate the grant program and your strategy (see chapter 3). Remember that in a spreadsheet you can insert a link to a file on your computer. If you don't move the file around, you can always access it for a quick view from the spreadsheet.

Next, you'll clean up the electronic files you leave behind for future reference. A decade ago you would have photocopied the letters and proposals, responses, reports, and canceled checks to a paper file and, if appropriate, logged them into a database. Now we capture those same materials electronically in the funder file and with subfiles for donor information and project applications. In the rush to move on to the next project, this can seem time consuming, but it will save you so much time when the grant announcement comes out and you find yourself reviewing the situation. This information is also important for tracking when you can next apply, maintaining an active relationship with the donor, and evaluating the results of your grant program.

So create, or keep, the file using the funder's name; then create a subfile for the year (presumably you'll apply again in a year, and that will be a different subfile). Then save, either as individual files or as subfiles (depending upon the complexity of the proposal), application package/final submitted materials, drafts, attachments, and resource documents. In the main file, you can leave the funder information, copies of emails with the funder or call notes, and a scan of the funder's response. Carefully delete many of the drafts, keeping those with director's edits or with important material that you've prepared but that didn't make the submitted letter or proposal. You may wish to use that text another time or in a follow-up to this funder. Keep a tidy file of the attachments, the CVs and letters of support, and the abstract and the table of contents, if they were requested; the budget form and any budget notes—whether submitted or for your own management purposes; and any other material specifically requested by the funder or allowed as an attachment, such as a previous year's report, or evaluation reports, sample materials, exhibit designs, or an objects list, for example. Then take a moment to fill out the "If We Get the Grant" form at the end of this chapter. It is the cheat sheet you will need to cognitively switch into grant mode as efficiently as possible when that grant does come in. Now you can close the file and move on.

There will not be much, if anything, to do with this application while you wait; still, many funders appreciate updates or special information during the consideration period, as long as the information relates to the proposal under consideration. If you have a critical update to share with the funder, go ahead. The mostly likely update would be a significant grant award from another funder if you reported it in your proposal as under consideration. Other possible updates might be some great and related journalistic coverage, or a change in the project design that affects something important to the funder: location, scope, or objective. Usually you won't have a reason other than an income update, so just wait patiently. If the announcement date passes, you can contact the funder and ask for an update only after it appears to you to be delayed by three weeks. Please don't ask, "Did you fund us?" Instead, explain that you understood the target date for announcements was (date), and since a few weeks have passed, you are contacting them to see whether you missed a message. Then leave it there.

Even if you are about to work on the next proposal, now is when you complete the "If We Get the Grant" form and update (or create) your grant Activity Report. The Activity Report is a list of applications submitted, awarded, and declined, by funder, for which projects, for how much, and the submittal date. This report should be completed quarterly at a minimum, and monthly for best practice. Share this with your staff and board so that they are aware of the funding activities and results. You can use this for your annual or semiannual grant program evaluation. The "If We Get the Grant" form is the way you will short-cut the start time if the grant comes in.

WHAT IF YOU GET A "NO"?

Darn. This is always tough. It never stops being tough, but you do develop patience with it, over time. You'll get the message in an email or a standard letter. Hopefully the funder will give you a reason that is more helpful than "We received many more applications than we could fund. Unfortunately, yours was not selected to receive funding." If the funder provides feedback, then use that information to decide if, when, and how to apply again. If the letter isn't informative, please wait at least three business days before calling. Explain that you applied in the last cycle and did not receive a grant; can you have ten minutes to speak to a program officer on how to best approach the funder again? If you get a "yes," then be prepared to refresh the program officer's memory with the basics of your organization and proposal—one sentence for each piece. Then listen carefully. At the conclusion, if it is not yet clear, ask how appropriate it would be to apply again. Then act accordingly.

WHEN YOU GET A "YES"

Celebrate! If ever "yes" ceases to be a cause for celebration, you should consider changing roles. This is a gift—a huge gift because it is someone else's money. Please pause and appreciate the importance of a financial gift, and celebrate the importance and effectiveness of the work you put into it. Then you can quickly grab the "If We Get the Grant" form to refresh your memory, and move on to your response.

Thank-Yous

First, review the guidelines for acknowledging the gift and reporting on the results. You will need this for the inevitable questions when you tell your boss and board about the announcement. Then tell any staff who will administer the grant so they can begin implementing the work as soon as the proposed timeline begins and the cash is in the bank. Within the week, send distinctly different written thank-you letters from the director and from the board chair, making sure the authors carefully personalize their messages. A generous gift requires a genuine thank-you. Then prepare to include the announcement on your web page and any other message format you use with members and the community. If this gift is appropriate for physical acknowledgment at your institution on a donor board or special installation, begin the process of including it.

Naples Botanical Garden Donor Wall with the title "A Dream Realized"
Courtesy of Sarah Sutton

Dorothy Molter saved broken paddles she found near her home in the Boundary Waters of Minnesota, repainting them for decoration. At her restored home, now a museum, the staff use a similar approach to recognize donors.
Courtesy of Jess Edberg

At the Visionary Art Museum, the donor wall is titled "Like a Fine Wine, Our Donors Fortify and Delight"
Courtesy of Sarah Sutton

Reporting

The role of the report is to reassure the donor that the funds were used properly, appropriately, and successfully. Many funders ask for specific kinds of reporting on the use of the funds and the results of the project. Be sure to note these formats and expectations before you begin the project so that you can comply fully and intelligently once you do. When the funder does not ask for a report, provide the information you find most appropriate in the format that works best for you. In most cases a single-page summary with numbers and text will do, plus simple support materials ranging from examples of students' work and quotes from participants to images of the program in progress and references to local newspaper coverage. Give the donor useful material for its annual report, on its website, or in conversation with other donors as appropriate.

If you encounter problems during the grant implementation process, you may need to call and speak with the funder. Let's say that the contractor for a major part of the project cannot fulfill his or her commitment. After you confirm all the whys and why-nots of this situation, identify a replacement, and then call to let the funder know that there must be a change and how you would like to proceed. The funder will let you know whether anything more formal than that call is required. The same applies if the project will take longer than expected, or if you lose one partner or a venue and must replace them with another. If the change affects cost, time, or implementation, then it's important to let the funder know. No one likes surprises, especially with their money.

If, as the project comes to completion, you experience different results than expected during the project, explain them appropriately in the report. Most funders are active learners who want to apply grantees' valuable lessons to other approaches and projects. They understand that there will be unforeseen events and unpredictable results. Who knows—the funder may be interested in supporting more programming to address these discoveries. No matter what, do not fail to report on what you did and to thank the donor, again, for its support. This is other people's money; steward it as carefully as if it were your own—both kinds are irreplaceable.

STAYING IN TOUCH AFTER THE FIRST GRANT

You *can* have a relationship with a funder without asking for money. In between funding, stay in touch with your foundation contact by sharing useful information on your organization and, possibly, the field. Twice a year is enough. Only send information they are not likely to see in

Grant Proposal Data and Next-Steps Reminders   Project Name:

If we don't get it

- ☐ Consider thanking funder, in writing, for their work in reviewing the proposal and giving you notice
- ☐ As appropriate, ask for a chance to discuss the proposal and a potential future application
- ☐ Attach, or record below, funder comments and response

If we do get it

- ☐ Director thanks the funder by phone and in paper or e-letter as appropriate
- ☐ Director thanks any endorsers by email
- ☐ A board member thanks the funder in writing
- ☐ Review and submit grant agreement if requested

Project Nickname

Funder Name

Submitter Name

Project Director

Submittal Date

Expected Notice

Start Date

Report Date/s

End Date

Response   Y / N

Request Amount

Funded Amount

Figure 9.1

Attach, physically or electronically:

- ☐ Project schedule
- ☐ Budget math notes and any estimates or proposal
- ☐ Consultant and contractor contact information

Implementation: Getting Started

- ☐ Inform staff, contractors, and consultants of the award
- ☐ Share proposal components with them as appropriate
- ☐ Establish any communication protocols and channels (BaseCamp, DropBox, Google, email).
- ☐ Schedule initial team meeting
- ☐ Review proposal
  - o Does the timeline still make sense?
  - o Do we need to order something promptly?
  - o Do we need to quickly schedule or reschedule a public event or program?

"If We Get the Grant" form

their own e-lists, e-newsletters, and professional memberships. You can invite them occasionally to join advisory boards, selection panels, or brainstorming sessions. In all cases, make sure the contact is relevant and useful for both sides. As genuine partners, you will each benefit in many ways.

CONGRATULATIONS! YOU HAVE BEEN AWARDED A GRANT!

On that glorious day when an award letter arrives, or your legislator calls to say it will, take the time to celebrate with your team. Go ahead and make sure they all know the grant came in, and thank them for their work. Let the director know (if you're not the director). Then inform your board chair, and write the first thank-you note. And write it down somewhere for others to notice and share in the celebration—this may be the staff bulletin board, an email to the board and staff, even a notice on your door in the staff room. Each grant really matters, so make sure that everyone knows and celebrates with you. Tomorrow you can retrieve the "If We Get the Grant" form, write a press release, and begin the work you hoped to do.

CHAPTER 10

How Do I Fit This into My Day?
or How Do I Accomplish More?

I bet your fundraising to-do list looks like this:

- find major sponsor for gala
- ask printer to donate the school program printing again
- figure out IMLS
- report to community foundation
- fund new school programs
- annual appeal
- someone to buy us a new copier?

That's a heck of a list. If this *is* what yours looks like, then I suggest some reframing just so that you can get started on it.

Each of those is an entire project, and all but the printing donation and the community foundation report are a whole flowchart of decision making away from being completed. The yes/no decisions in those projects require strategizing that belongs not on a to-do list, but back in chapter 3 where you set out your initial strategy. First, put each of those complex items through a strategic assessment. You can consider adding them to your to-do list *after* framing each step to make them more manageable.

To increase your efficiency and peace of mind, break all your fundraising responsibilities into activities you can reasonably fit into your day. Let's examine a proposal-preparation project and make it more manageable and clearer as to your efforts and results. Here's how to turn "figure out IMLS" into a series of to-dos. Table 10.1

reflects process (to-do) and product (why/what/how) so that you can get organized. Just as the project you're writing about has outputs and outcomes for each activity, so does the project that is your proposal-writing process.

Yes, your day still has too many to-dos competing for your limited time, but it will be much easier to fit in these smaller, specific pieces than to tackle a huge, still-vague project. Inevitably your attention to this proposal will become more focused, possibly pressured, as the deadline looms closer. Breaking up the list into manageable chunks will help you manage the stressful part of the run-up to submittal.

Table 10.1.   Making the To-Do List Manageable

To-Do	Why/What/How
Team meeting: brainstorm IMLS options	Team recommends two or three projects to the director
Meet with team and director on final choice	Identify responsibilities and unanswered questions, set team schedule
Team meeting to draft logic model and budget	Build team ownership, improve project
Update SAM & grants.gov, organizational profile, strategic plan page, Form 242S	Finish the easy parts, feel like you're getting ready, simplify submittal day
Outline the proposal, start naming partners	Get ahead on actions that take lead time: confirm consultants and partners, collect CVs and letters when roles are defined
Team meeting: review logic model, budget	Confirm team ownership, answer almost all design questions
Write the first draft	Then share with team for review
Team meeting three days later	Refine project, identify missing pieces
Write second draft	Then share with director for comments, and with team for corrections and gaps
Request letters and estimates	To finish the budget, begin collecting proposal pieces
Team meeting three days later	Keep the whole group waiting in the room if some need to call/email for missing pieces
Third draft with near-final budget, logic model	Share with director
Final draft	Share with director—one day turnaround
Share all pages with proofreader	Make sure you have a professional product
Submit ahead of deadline, and when the office is quiet	Limit the interruptions, and the chances of technology delays from system overload

WHEN THE LIST IS TOO LONG, TOO COMPLEX

What do you do, though, if you have multiple proposals due in a similar time frame and the lists are so long as to be counterproductive? The details can get overwhelming, and a few may get dropped. One way to manage the confusion is to shift from tackling multiple projects simultaneously to tackling one specific aspect of each one under way simultaneously. In one work session, you might prepare the text sections such as organization history or audience, or the budgets, for two proposals. Half the challenge of getting this done is the shift to starting on a new section of the proposal. Once you're started, you can use that momentum to complete work on more than one. The idea is that your brain is already in that mode of thinking, so it has the energy and focus to work most efficiently.

There are cognitive reasons for the difficulties of getting started on a new part of the work at hand. In the processes of switching from one task or goal to another, or from one mental process or set of rules to another, your brain has a switching delay that consumes productive time. If you switch both goals and rules as you move from a creative task on one proposal to a logic-driven task on another, then you may lose productivity by even more than double the amount compared to a switch between activities with shared goals and rules. So, if after writing the IMLS narrative you sit down to fill out the Johnson Foundation audience information, you will lose more time in transition than if you worked on the narratives for both, or the audience information for both, in sequence.[1]

If you have to format photographs and find attachments, try doing it for all three proposals in sequence before turning to other proposal work. If you're chasing all the support letters for a number of projects at once, take care to make the list of calls and emails along with a progress chart. This chart is for checking off actions, such as when you've called and spoken with someone (and the result) or when you've left a phone or email message. Don't forget to include the do-next step on this chart if you cannot yet cross this off your to-do list.

When you're in the mental mode of logic models and budgets, and you are identifying numbers, materials, and people for the purpose of calculating importance and costs, try tackling a logic model and budget for two proposals in succession. You will be able to apply the same cognitive "rules" in your brain for both projects, and you can move relatively easily from one completed project to the next because they have a similar goal. While you're working on one budget, as you come across information related to one of the other projects, save it electronically or in print to shortcut the process on the next proposal. Or while checking flight or mileage costs for one project, you might as well check the flight or mileage costs for the other two since you'll be exploring the same websites and making the same type of calculations. This idea also applies to the case-making creative writing of a few projects. If you're writing the organizational history, get one fully updated, and then tweak the others to reflect additional information more in tune with their focus. Though the content will shift some among them, the processes you are using and content you are working on will at least have similarities and be limited to one type of information to manage at once.

If your job has responsibilities beyond fundraising, you can apply the same principles across types of projects. Try chunking activities with similar goals and rules regardless of their part in fundraising, maintenance, or volunteer management. So, if you're working on the annual report for the year, consider immediately updating the stock version of the organizational history text and the audience data regularly used in proposals. If you're writing copy for a program or exhibit that you will need to fund, at least capture the copy as material for the proposals; maybe you can even flow right from sketching out the storyboard and sample copy to describing the project in a proposal. The idea is to tackle similar projects in sequence so that one set of work flows smoothly into another. The time and stress you save will improve your production on many levels.

REFRAMING "FIT THIS IN" TO BE "ACCOMPLISH MORE"

Let's make one more shift. We've reframed to-do projects into to-do lists; we've chunked to-dos by grouping activities with similar cognitive goals and rules to give your brain a break and make you more efficient—now let's reframe attitude and energy. The goal is not to "fit this in" to your day but to "accomplish more" in your role at the institution. Often the complex work of organizing a project and writing about it gets shunted to the side as time-sensitive issues and urgent situations invade your orderly approach. It's a fight to keep fundraising as an equally urgent priority. If all you do is try to fit in this work, then you fuel the feeling that fundraising is separate from other important work. You miss the opportunity to demonstrate how your work is not separate from the success of other aspects of the museum's work but a well-integrated part of it. It is as important as curatorial, educational, and promotional work, so treat it that way. Without it, the organization cannot accomplish more. Funding in the future may become the go/no-go point for a valuable project, for a person's continued job, or for a program that drives the mission to a new level. When you look at your day, ask yourself, "What's most important for moving us forward?" Do that first. Fundraising should be that most important thing at least twice a week, if not more often, depending upon your role and the organization's mission.

MAKING EACH ACTIVITY EASIER

So, how do you leverage your capacity to move your organization forward? Every job can benefit from review for improvement, so here we'll explore some tools and approaches that can help you maintain a strong, thoughtful program even with competition for your time.

Do-Next List

This kind of list addresses the problem of cognitive delays when you switch tasks in writing. A do-next list will help you be more efficient. It helps if you do more than fundraise at your organization, and for each proposal. As you complete one task and move on to something else, or go home for the evening, take time to make a note to yourself of the next most appropriate activity to tackle as you research funders for a project, work on a proposal, or determine where to work next on a writing task. It's like a bookmark. It doesn't go on your daily to-do list, but when you return to the project, this prompt will help you get started more easily. Otherwise you would have to review your last work to update yourself, and then remake the decision of what to do next. Put the do-next task on a sticky note and paste it right where you'll open the file—whether it's a paper or electronic file.

Tracking Funder Data

In chapter 2 there was information on the funder search process. Now let's think about holding on to the information you need on funders you plan to approach, and think about scheduling those approaches. Whatever resources you use to find your supporters, when you turn to reviewing the funder list to find a potential project match, rather than relying on memory, you will appreciate being able to see a short prompt on their interests and basic details.

- If you own access to a funder database, such as the Foundation Directory Online or the regional grantmakers' database, then you can just search for them in the database or in the files you save in the online program.
- If you have limited access to a database and/or you collect funders from other sources, then keep an in-house search system for re-calling your funders and your prospects (the ones you hope to apply to, or think someday you might be able to apply to).
- If you have membership software, likely there is a grant and major gift module you can adapt or activate.
- If you don't have a database, or do not wish to use one, you can make this work with a spreadsheet or a paper file.

Choose whatever suits your resources and the way you process information. No off-the-shelf software will fit you like something you design; whatever you design will need to change, so please do not dream of perfection. You can always consider asking for a fundraising software system from your donors. Online discount database access for nonprofits is an option, but be sure to review the financial obligations after the initial enrollment period. None are free or very low-cost.

If you have twenty to thirty active funders, you can keep this all in a spreadsheet with good file notes. Focus on capturing the data unique to your relationship with the funder, taking care not to re-create easily accessible online data. Start with an Active Funders sheet with headers to reflect funder name, program alignment, contact information, due dates, request range, and notice dates. Set up additional headers to reflect the proposal you submit by topic, frequent amount, submittal date, and the funder response. If there are notes to recommend the approach for subsequent applications, add them as well. Many spreadsheets allow you to create a link in a field that takes the user to a connected document or website. Keep the donor's website link here, as well as internal computer links to past proposals, any file notes, a copy of the award or response letter, and copies of reports. If you use this approach, though, remember not to move these files from the linked location in the future. It is helpful to set up an electronic folder that holds all the documents linked to the spreadsheet for a fiscal year.

On a second page, you can keep information on the prospects. These are the ones you think are a good fit but for which there is no project match yet, the ones you will contact once you have reached some necessary milestones, and ones that fund similar organizations but do not fund you yet. Keeping them here at least means you are prompted to review them when you start your next search. Keep just the basics here—mission, program, audience, effect, grant range, and generalized deadlines. The detailed information for inactive funders will change by the time you need to reexamine them, so don't spend your valuable time on minutiae. Even the information on funders you track in the spreadsheet or database will need to be refreshed, so design more for tracking your actions related to the funder, knowing that you will be checking online for updates to the donor's institutional interests and details.

Deadline Schedule

The episodic nature of proposal writing and grant awards means the grant process gets all revved up, only to sit for a bit until the revving starts again. That inertia followed by a scramble is inefficient and uncomfortable for those trying to work within it. Reviewing your deadlines and announcements quarterly will help you smooth out the mix of project planning and proposal writing within the confines of those dates.

You can organize deadline sequences chronologically in the spread-sheets, or data-sort for them if you keep the funders listed alphabetically. Keep a shorthand list somewhere else, too. Then, when you sit down at the beginning of each quarter and map out likely proposals for the next four quarters, make sure the spreadsheet and a master calendar reflect the same material. For the funders who have no deadlines, put them in the chart at the top of their fiscal year, and plan to apply as early as you can in their year in case their funds run out.

A wall calendar with grant dates is an easy way to keep deadlines front of mind and helps others remember what you're working on. Some proposal writers keep schedules of projects, deadlines, and report due dates on dedicated whiteboards or posters with sticky notes. Others have grants calendars on their computer desktops or on their electronic calendars. I keep just the basic information on small stickies, set in columns by month, stuck inside a neon-colored and otherwise empty file folder *on my desk*. I can always find the folder and look up the next proposal in less than ten seconds.

Triage Your Applications

Once more, the premier strategy for accomplishing more is making sure that you're working on the right proposals. So, revisit the grant tiers from chapter 3 and make sure you are using the criteria you've developed for identifying good funder-project matches. Use this to support your decision making when you really cannot take on another proposal and must decide which to cut.

This is helpful when others come to you with a list of potential funders, or even just one or two, to add to your list. First, remember two things: one, that it can be helpful to have others searching along with you; and two, that they've selected these funders because they are not sure or don't think you've applied and they're not sure why you haven't. You'll have to explain the why or why not of your selection. To shortcut this in the future, share your evaluation criteria with your board and volunteers so they can winnow their lists to only viable *and* valuable prospects. You can share a cheat sheet of criteria you've developed or the Hierarchy of Funder Needs as tools to guide their process of vetting a funder before suggesting them.

Here's how you might explain this:

We have a working list of important criteria for good matches with our
funders. There are so many nonprofits also looking for support that only
the strongest matches are considered. To be sure we are considered, we
will only apply to a foundation or corporation if, first, we have documentation that they accept unsolicited proposals, then, at a minimum,
our programs and the funder's guidelines match on each of these criteria:
organizational mission, target audience (geographic and demographic),
and program goals or results.

Next, the project-funder match must also fit at least two of these
four criteria:

- The project has to be a priority (a funder and a deadline aren't
  enough of a reason to spend the time to write a grant).
- Someone on our staff or the board has a personal connection to
  the funder, or the staff has spoken to the foundation staff and been
  encouraged.
- The amount of the likely award is worth the proposal effort.
- The proposal is already prepared, so to send this makes sense and
  still only takes two hours of work.

If you feel your board and staff have a good understanding of the
process and likely results, you can take this opportunity to re-create
criteria together each year as you set your goals. This helps them
understand your focus and effort and shares the responsibility. It also
creates educated partners in the fundraising process. You will need
them to reach out to their contacts, to make a fundraising request, or to
host a funder tour someday. By preparing them, you are preparing to
accomplish more.

SO, WHAT'S NEXT?

Other than the next grant proposal on the deadline list, what's next is
monitoring the grant profession and being prepared for coming changes
in the field. Just as any profession matures, so does philanthropy. Our

job, as professionals, is to continue to improve our understanding of philanthropy and respond to its nuances as efficiently and effectively as possible. In the next decade it *is* very likely that private foundation giving will increase; so will demand for those funds and the complexities of accepting them.

- As some legacy foundations choose to spend down their corpus, to sunset their foundations, large amounts of funding may appear for a few years in certain categories, and then end. This is good in the short term but a challenge for planning for future grant cycles and potential income.
- New foundations based on new-business wealth, and those that expand giving through socially responsible philanthropy, will create more funding opportunities and add money to the funder pool.
- Some funders have chosen to delegate a portion of their funds to intermediary organizations particularly experienced in a distinct service area such as the environment. This is a new practice that is likely to increase as areas of interest benefit from research based on the results of these early grants. This degree of separation between the funder and the recipient makes it very difficult to use the traditional approach of cultivating relationships that may lead to funding in the future.
- The no-strings-attached approach will no longer be the rule. We will continue to see more new funders choose to participate directly in the granting process and oversee those awards. They will name highly specific interests that narrow the funding options for those left outside the target area. They will create very specific requests for proposals that predetermine the design of the outcomes. This may be as specific as research into flood mitigation approaches for historic properties and evaluation of STEAM programming in museum-school programs. Such specificity will be a problem for applicants with very specific foci that were acceptable under previous, more umbrella-like guidelines but now fall outside those guidelines.
- Still, I see increased participation by funders as an additional gift to the museum, that of intellect and experience. Funders have deep knowledge from their giving experience, broad findings stored in

the reports they commission, and expertise among their staff and peers, of which we can only dream.

These changes require us to examine and improve our practice in ways that make our work even more professional and accountable than it had been in the last decades. Some of us will be forced to review missions created ten or twenty years ago, and to find more relevant alignments and language. This sophistication can result in even more effective work by our museums and sites.

Reading this is one step toward that goal. Maybe in chapter 1, "Understanding the System," you discovered that it is time to mature from easy, "family" grants to more complex grants based entirely on institutional alignment. Perhaps chapter 2, "Finding a Funder; Ensuring the Match," forced you to reexamine your mission when you realized too few funders' interests aligned with your work. Or, when you read chapter 3 about institutional strategies and this chapter about fitting this into your day, maybe you realized that the best next step was a game-changing partnership with a strong ally.

Whatever it is, please share what you learn with others around you. By continuing to learn from practice, and from conversations with peers and funders, each of us can significantly strengthen our organizations and the credibility of the field. Raising money through grants is a team sport. I'm glad to have you working with me on behalf of museums.

NOTE

1. "Multitasking: Switching Costs," American Psychology Association, March 20, 2006, accessed July 15, 2017, http://www.apa.org/research/action /multitask.aspx.

Bibliography

Alford, Katie, Darryl Tocker, Laura L. Duty, and Gary Smith. "Thinking Like a Donor: Down-to-Earth Advice from Foundations on Seeking Funds." Panel presentation at the "I AM History" American Association for State and Local History Annual Conference, Austin, Texas, September 6–9, 2017.

American Psychology Association. "Multitasking: Switching Costs." March 20, 2006. Accessed July 15, 2017. http://www.apa.org/research/action/multitask.aspx.

Andalusia Farm. "About Us." Accessed April 7, 2017. http://andalusiafarm.org.

Blithewold. "About the Estate." Accessed April 7, 2017. http://www.blithewold.org/about/the-estate/.

Brophy, Sarah S. *Is Your Museum Grant-Ready? Assessing Your Organization's Potential for Funding.* Lanham, MD: AltaMira Press, 2005.

Colorado Historical Society, Office of Archaeology and Historic Preservation. *Museum Buildings, Sites and Structures on the Colorado State Register of Historic Properties.* 2008. http://www.historycolorado.org/sites/default/files/files/OAHP/crforms_edumat/pdfs/1639.pdf.

Deacon, Goodwin, and Ken Ristine. *Grantsmanship for the Genius: A Master Grantwriter and a Veteran Funder Reveal the Keys to Winning Grants.* Nashville, TN: For the Genius Press, 2016.

Dumbarton House. "Dumbarton House Receives 2013 Mayor's Sustainability Award." Accessed October 19, 2017. http://dumbartonhouse.org/2013-mayors-sustainability-award.

Foundation Center. "Key Facts on U.S. Foundations, 2014." Accessed August 25, 2017. http://foundationcenter.org/gainknowledge/research/keyfacts2014/foundation-focus.html.

Genegabus, Jason. "Shaping Hearts & Minds." *Honolulu Star-Advertiser Sunday Magazine,* June 18, 2017.

GrantCraft. *When Projects Flounder*. New York: Ford Foundation, 2003.

History Relevance. "Value of History." Accessed August 25, 2017. https://www.historyrelevance.com/value-history-statement/.

Independent Sector. "The Sector's Economic Impact." Accessed September 22, 2016. https://www.independentsector.org/economic_role.

Internal Revenue Service. "7.27.16 Taxes on Foundation Failure to Distribute Income." Accessed October 6, 2017. https://www.irs.gov/irm/part7/irm_07-027-016.

Lyall, Sarah. "Off the Beat and Into a Museum: Art Helps Police Officers Learn to Look." *New York Times*, April 26, 2016. https://www.nytimes.com/2016/04/27/arts/design/art-helps-police-officers-learn-to-look.html?_r=0.

National Council of Nonprofits. "State Law Nonprofit Audit Requirements: Does Your State's Law Require an Independent Audit?" Accessed April 7, 2017. https://www.councilofnonprofits.org/nonprofit-audit-guide/state-law-audit-requirements.

Phillips, Frances. "Crafting a Competitive LOI." Webinar, Foundation Center training event, GrantSpace, May 24, 2016.

Urban Institute. "The Nonprofit Sector in Brief 2015: Public Charities Giving and Volunteering." Accessed August 25, 2017. https://www.urban.org/sites/default/files/publication/72536/2000497-The-Nonprofit-Sector-in-Brief-2015-Public-Charities-Giving-and-Volunteering.pdf.

Wineburg, Samuel S. *Historical Thinking and Other Unnatural Acts: Charting the Future of Teaching the Past*. Philadelphia: Temple University Press, 2001.

Wineburg, Samuel S. "Historical Thinking Matters." Accessed August 25, 2017. https://sheg.stanford.edu/htm.

Index

501(c)(3) letter, 7

AAM. *See* American Alliance of Museums
AAP. *See* Artifact Assessment Program
AASLH. *See* American Association for State and Local History
Abbe Museum, 96–97, 97*f*
acceptance, 154, 155*f*–56*f*, 157
accreditation, 77–80
activities, for logic model, 102, 103*t*; sample, 108
advisors, quality of, 76–77
Alford, Katie, 32
American Alliance of Museums (AAM), 19; accreditation from, 77
American Association for State and Local History (AASLH), 32, 49, 78
Americans for the Arts, 80
AOR. *See* Authorized Organization Representative
applications: sequence of, planning for, 40–45; triaging, 168–69
Artifact Assessment Program (AAP), 19

aspirational funders, 42
attachments: for electronic submissions, 144–45; for federal proposals, 147
audience: characteristics of, 67–69; distinctive, 69–70; future, 70–71; matching, 26–27, 29–30; of proposal, 138–39; and value to funders, 63*b*, 67–71
audit requirements, 87–88
Authorized Organization Representative (AOR), 116, 145–46

balance sheet. *See* statement of position
benefits: maximizing, 93; and value to funders, 63*b*, 73–75, 73*t*
Blithewold Mansion, Gardens and Arboretum, 78, 82–83
board: policies and, 37–38; proposal on, 140; and value to funders, 83; written ethical standards for, 85
boilerplate materials, 119–20; caution with, 140*b*–41*b*
budgets, 110–12; categories in, 111–12; for grants, 38–39

government grants, 18–21; agency
services, 19; process for, 20–21;
timeframe for writing proposals,
116–17
grants, 1–5, 35–59; foundation
process for, 15–18; future of,
169–71; goals for, 42–45;
planning for, 40–45; policies
and procedures, 35–38, 84–85;
prestigious, in institutional history
section, 79–80; readiness for,
checklist on, 61–62, 63*b*–64*b*;
role in institution, 35; system
of, 7–21
grants.gov, 4, 20, 145–48;
Workspace, 146, 148

How House, 47–48, 47*f*, 48*f*, 72

"If We Get the Grant" form,
152–53, 158*f*
Image Permanence Institute, 96
IMLS. *See* Institute of Museum
and Library Services
impact: matching, 30; maximizing,
92–94; significance and
appropriateness of, 72; and value
to funders, 63*b*, 71–75
infrastructure anxiety, and operating
grants, 9–10
innovative edge, 95–97
inputs, for logic model, 102, 103*t*;
sample, 107–8
Institute of Museum and Library
Services (IMLS), 2, 19, 21,
47–48, 50, 52, 71, 78, 80, 147
institution: accreditation/qualification
of, 77–80; quality of, and value to
funders, 82–88

institutional comparables, 66
institutional evolution: examples of,
54–56; tiers of, 49–54, 58–59;
and value to funders, 62
institutional history: versus mission
statement, 140*b*; in proposal,
139, 140*b*
institutional strategy, 35–59
institutional weakness, signs of, 82
intermediary organizations, 170
Internal Revenue Service (IRS):
501(c)(3) letter, 7; Form 990s, 28
introduction, of proposal, 138
investment: financial and
management practices and, 63*b*,
82–88; maximizing, 92–94;
return on, 58
invitation, for foundation
applications, 15
IRS. *See* Internal Revenue Service

John Hair Cultural Center and
Museum, 118–19, 119*f*
Johnstown Center, 123*b*–24*b*

Kawa'a, Earl, 102, 104
Kellogg Foundation, 80
Kresge Foundation, 42

lagging indicators, 43–44
Lawrence (Charles) House, 122*b*–23*b*
leading indicators, 43
letter of inquiry/interest (LOI):
versus concept letter, 127–35;
for continuing project, 120–21;
with existing content, 119–20;
format for, 128–31; length of,
130, 132–33; for operating
support, 131–32; sample,

About the Author

Sarah Sutton leads Sustainable Museums, a consultancy in grant program development and environmental sustainability for museums, zoos, gardens, aquariums and historic sites. She has nearly thirty years of experience focused on strategic grants program development. She coaches and consults nationally and internationally, and she teaches online. She helps clients strategically design or redesign their pursuit of grant funds and sustain a year-round grants pipeline. In her webinars, conference presentations, and individual consulting, she helps all levels of proposal writers prepare excellent proposals to support their institutions' missions.

In 2008 she began raising money for environmental sustainability at museums, zoos, gardens, and historic sites. She found that it added value to each institution's work and their proposals to funders. She particularly loves the challenge of federal grant applications. Some of her personal-best awards have come from the Kresge Foundation, Fidelity Foundation, the Cummings Foundation's $100k for 100 program, the National Endowment for the Humanities Challenge Grant Program, the National Science Foundation, and the Institute of Museum and Library Services. In her writing she emphasizes the importance of strong project design, a personal voice in the proposal, and a no-jargon approach. She wrote the first edition of *Is Your Museum Grant-Ready?* in 2005. Back then she was Sarah Brophy; now she writes as Sarah Sutton.